# PHOBIAS

## Overview on 165 Psychological Phobias

**Dr.Y. Narasimha Raja**

Ph.D., MBA, M.Sc. Psychology, M. Com, MTM
Assistant Professor – School of Management
Presidency University, Bangalore.

**Mrs.Y. Sree Lakshmi**

M.Sc. Psychology, B. Tech

The author articulated this book, with his research, various sources of books, electronic media, Social media, magazines, anecdotes, stories, journals, Interviewing with various experts, other speakers, and seminar participants. Primary and Secondary data have been considered. If any resemblance regarding the topic is purely coincidence as many examples and subject details have been collected from various sources. Regrettably, sources were not always renowned or available; hence, it became impractical to provide an accurate recognition.

**MRP: Indian Rupees (INR) 300/-**

**ISBN: 9798890022592**

**Publishers: Notion Press**

**800, West El Camino Real #180,California USA 94040**

**Notion Press Media Pvt Ltd,**

No.50, Chettiyar Agaram Main Road,Vanagaram,

**Chennai, 600095, Contact** +9144 46315631

Email : publish@notionpress.com

web: www.notionpress.com

# Contents

# Preface

*"Everything is Easy, when you are Crazy,*
*but nothing is Easy, when you are Lazy "*
*–Swami Vivekananda*

This quote has inspired the author to keep their maximum efforts to write this book.

*In this book, 165 Phobias have been emphasized that human being can overcome.*

It provides a broad range of information concisely and in an easy-to-read way. I assure, if these principles are applied in our practical life situation, we can defiantly view positive results within a fast span of time.

This book is written in simple English and self-explanatory for the purpose of readers' empowerment.

*Never think I have nothing,*
*Never think I have everything,*
*but, always think*
*I have something & I can achieve anything*

# About Author

Dr. Y. Narasimha Raja is an International Trainer, Psychologist, Author, Coach, Mentor, Motivational speaker, counsellor and subject matter expert in his domain. He holds a Ph.D. degree in Management studies and multiple degrees that include Master of Business Administration, Master of Science in Psychology, Master of Commerce, and Master of Tourism Management.

He has more than 19 years of vast corporate experience in India & abroad. He has served various global corporate companies as Lead HR. He has a proven track of delivering responsibilities Professional merits

Professional Awards & certifications

- "Best HR Practitioner " certifications from Construction Industry Development Council (CIDC) during – Vishwakarma Awards for the year 2019 associated body of NITI Agog
  *(Formerly called Planning Commission of India).*
- National Prime Author Award -2021 by the Foxclues
- India Influence Award -2021 Best Corporate Trainer – Learning & Development – Organized By The The Crazy Tales fy 2021

- In his tenure, he has received several certifications for his performance from his organization viz *Merit of HR Operational Excellence, Well-done, systems & process, Great Job, Extra mile and many more.*
- He is certified as "Indian Management Styles" from the *Bangalore University* for the year 2002"

Personal Awards & Certifications

- 2002 Best Citizen Award - Andhra Pradesh Police
- 2000 Represented India South Asian Youth camp
- 1999 Represented India South Asian Youth Camp
- 2001 Pre Republic Parade – NSS
- 2002 N.C.C –Army Wing – C Certificate

Book Publications:

1. Highly Effective Parenting Skills
2. Highly Effective Teaching Skills
3. The best & smart Teaching techniques
4. Happy Parenting Skills
5. Stage Fear – 101 Techniques to overcome the stage fear.
6. Highly effective Public Speaking Skills
7. Phobias-Overview on 165 phobias

His lectures, articles, seminars have created a tremendous impact on people and shown them the path to achieve success. Apart from his corporate experience, currently, he is serving as an Assistant professor at Presidency University, Bangalore.

# About Mrs. Y Sree Lakshmi

Mrs. Yagnamurthy Sree Lakshmi is a self driven enthusiastic individual.

She holds a Bachelor's degree in Electrical and Electronics engineering and Master of sciences in Psychology. She has 17 years of Corporate experience and as part of her job she has met many individuals across the globe and finds human psychology a very interesting and fascinating subject. She is an author, trainer, researcher and counsellor.

She is a mother of two wonderful boys whom she considers as a source of inspiration to learn new things everyday and dedicates her psychology degree to them.

She believes in the motto of live by example and would like to help people overcome the psychological stress in their everyday life.

# Readers note

The author has kept his highest efforts in writing this book. He respects all the readers and their feelings. He believes that all the readers are positive attitude icons. This book is written in simple English a self-explanatory mode for the purpose of reareader'spowerment.

*He sees, the readers to be Swan bird,*
*Who can separate milk from a mixture of water?*

If you find any errors in this book, kindly forgive and observe the goodness of this book.

*Let us be a player in life, who runs for the goal & not a referee who looks for the faults*

Language is just a means of communication; author has seen many thought provoking incidents, which has made him to pen down this book to spread awareness among us. Please extend positive thoughts &awareness of this book in the society.

With you and for you

**Dr.Y.Narasimha Raja**
**Mrs. Y.Sree Lakshmi**

# Learning sessions with the Author

My sincere thanks goes to all the readers and their family members. Having trust on me and this subject book.

I guarantee this book will drive help to bring trust & happiness in family. Reading the book is not enough and it should come in practicality.

I am selling this book for a nominal cost, my primary intention is not to earn monetary profit from this book instead I believe in benefitting the reader out of this book.

As a value addition to the readers, I will be imparting learning sessions by modes of videos, email, and Whatsapp with the readers. To avail of these services, readers are requested to get connect with the author.

For Training, consultation, seminars get connect

**Dr.Y.Narasimha Raja**
**Mrs. Y.Sree Lakshmi**

Email: ynr.phd@gmail.com; Web : www.ynraja.com

WhatsApp: +91- 8073205840

# Introduction to Phobia

A phobia is a persistent, uncontrolled fear of a certain thing, circumstance, or action. A person may go to considerable efforts to avoid the cause of this phobia if it becomes too unbearable. An emotional breakdown or panic attack is one possible reaction. This panic comes suddenly, is powerful, and lasts for many minutes. When there is no actual risk, no danger occurs.

A phobia is a form of anxiety illness that makes a person feel intense, unreasonable anxiety about a circumstance, a living being, a location, or an item. When someone has a phobia, they frequently plan their lives to steer clear of what they see as hazardous. The threat that is envisioned is bigger than any harm that the terror-causing factor actually poses.

Phobias are mental diseases that can be diagnosed. When the root of their phobia is exposed, the person will feel extreme anguish. They may struggle to operate regularly as a result, and it may even trigger panic episodes.

# Causes of Phobias

Several elements could make it more likely that a phobia will manifest:

1. Genetics
2. Cultural Aspects
3. Environmental Aspects

### 1. Genetics:

According to research, some phobias may run in families.

For instance, identical twins raised apart and in different places could experience the same phobias. However, a lot of phobia sufferers don't have any family members who also have the condition.

### 2. Cultural aspects

Some phobias are exclusive to certain cultural groups. Taijin Kyofusho, a social phobia that almost exclusively affects Japanese people, is one example. This is a worry about hurting or offending people in social settings. It differs significantly from a classic form of social anxiety disorder when the sufferer fears being publicly humiliated or ashamed in front of others. So, it is plausible that culture contributes in some way to the emergence of phobias.

### 3. Environmental and behavioural influences:

Several phobias are founded on actual occurrences that people may or may not consciously recall. For instance, being attacked as a young child may be the cause of a dog fear. Teenage shyness or bullying in childhood might lead to social anxiety disorder. Most likely, a combination of these conditions must exist in order for a phobia to manifest. Before a firm conclusion can be drawn, more investigation is needed.

# List of Phobias

## 1. Achluophobia- Fear of the dark

Children frequently experience a fear of the dark, as do adults to varying degrees. Fear of something like nighttime darkness can also be a fear of potential or perceived threats disguised by the darkness rather than just the darkness itself.

A certain amount of fear of the dark is normal, particularly throughout a child's developmental stage. The majority of observers claim that fear of the dark rarely appears before the age of two. Scotophobia is the name for a person's fear of the dark that gets so bad that it is considered abnormal.

**Signs & symptoms**

- Being uneasy in any darkly lit setting
- Not wanting to go out at night
- refusing to leave the house at night, displaying physiological signs such as an accelerated heart rate, apparent shivering, and even feeling sick when compelled to spend time in the dark.
- Need a nightlight for sleep?
- Attempting to flee from dimly lit spaces

- If someone attempts to get you to spend time in the dark, you may become defensive or upset.
- A compulsion to spend the evenings indoors

**Causes**

- ✓ Fear of unknown threats lurking in the dark may not be tied to darkness itself (which is why horror and suspense movies often use darkness as a way to scare viewers).
- ✓ Lack of security and confidence may also contribute to this, particularly if you tend to have more frequent nighttime phobias when you're alone.

## 2. Acousticophobia - Fear of Loud sounds.

It is about the fear of loud sounds. For the aversion to specific sounds, such as eating, coughing, or alarms, see Misophonia. For the fear of making or taking phone calls, see Telephone phobia.

### Signs / Symptoms

- Heavy breathing and panic episodes are two common responses when balloons explode.
- In addition to experiencing headaches, the victim gets anxious to leave the loud noise's source. Hyperacusis, a high sensitivity to loud noises, may also be connected to, the cause of, or mistaken with it.
- A severe case of misophonia has been proposed to be referred to as phonophobia.

### Causes

- ✓ Ligyrophobics could be fearful of things like computer speakers or fire sirens that might suddenly create loud noises.

- ✓ When using a device like a home theatre system, computer, television, or CD player, the user may want to turn the volume all the way down before doing anything that would cause the speakers to emit sound.
- ✓ This will allow them to turn up the volume of the speakers to a level that is comfortable to listen to once the command to produce sound is given.
- ✓ Due to the loud instruments, such as drums, they might avoid parades and carnivals. Many phobics acquire agoraphobia as loud music is often played at joyous events. Other people who are ligyrophobic avoid any occasions where fireworks will be released.

# 3.Acrophobia-Fear of Heights

A fear or phobia of heights that is severe or unreasonable, even when one is not very far up, is known as acrophobia. It belongs to a group of distinct phobias termed "space and motion discomfort" that have a lot in common with one another in terms of their origins and available therapies. The fear of falling is a common natural fear that most individuals have when exposed to heights. Conversely, those who are unafraid of such exposure are considered to have a head for heights.

**Psychological symptoms:-**

- Feeling intense fear and anxiety when thinking about, looking at, or being in high places.
- Fearing that something negative will happen in a high place, such as falling or being trapped in a high place.
- Feeling a strong desire to escape if you're in a high place.

**Causes:-**

- ✓ Walking up a flight of stairs.
- ✓ Being on a ladder.
- ✓ Using a multi-level parking garage.
- ✓ Being on or crossing over a bridge.
- ✓ Being on a rollercoaster.
- ✓ Standing near a balcony or at the top of a building.

# 4. Aerophobia -fear of aircraft or flying

A fear or phobia of heights that is severe or unreasonable, even when one is not very far up, is known as acrophobia. It belongs to a group of distinct phobias termed "space and motion discomfort" that have a lot in common with one another in terms of their origins and available therapies. The fear of falling is a common natural fear that most individuals have when exposed to heights. Conversely, those who are unafraid of such exposure are considered to have a head for heights.

**Psychological symptoms**

- Feeling intense fear and anxiety when thinking about, looking at, or being in high places.
- Fearing that something negative will happen in a high place, such as falling or being trapped in a high place.
- Feeling a strong desire to escape if you're in a high place.

**Causes:-**

- Walking up a flight of stairs.
- Being on a ladder.
- Using a multi-level parking garage.
- Being on or crossing over a bridge.
- Being on a rollercoaster.

- Standing near a balcony or at the top of a building.
- Looking out a window of a tall building.

Aerophobia is an extreme fear of air travel. Afrophobic may suffer fear during many flight-related events, such as takeoff, landing, or being trapped within the aircraft.

The inability to board an aeroplane or other flying object while in flight, such as a helicopter, is referred to as fear of flying.It is also known as aviophobia, aerophobia, flight phobia, pteromechanophobia, and flying anxiety (although aerophobia also means a fear of draughts or of fresh air).

Aviophobia, sometimes known as "aerophobia," is a fear of flying. A fear of flying may have its roots in infancy or may develop as an adult as a result of numerous triggers.

A particular phobia called, "aerophobia" is characterised by a fear of flying or air travel.

Despite the fact that statistics show that flying is really safer than other modes of transportation like the car and train, many people nevertheless have a fear of flying.

The most severe symptoms may include panic attacks or vomiting at the mere sight or mention of an aeroplane or air travel.

# 5.Agoraphobia

Fear of locations and circumstances that might result in panic, helplessness, or shame. Agoraphobia is a kind of anxiety disorder that frequently appears following one or more panic attacks.Among the symptoms are anxiety and aversion to environments and circumstances that could arouse emotions of panic, entrapment, helplessness, or shame.

Agoraphobia is a mental and behavioral illness; more particularly, it is an anxiety condition that is characterized by feelings of anxiety in circumstances like open areas, public transportation, retail establishments, or even just being outside one's house. These circumstances could cause a panic attack. In extreme circumstances, people could lose the ability to function outside of their houses.

Fear that there is no quick method to get out or assistance if the anxiety worsens is what makes people anxious. Agoraphobics frequently struggle to feel secure in any public setting, particularly in areas where large groups congregate. You might think you need a buddy or family to accompany you when you go out in public.

**Signs / Symptoms :**

- Fear of: is one of the typical symptoms of agoraphobia.
- Leaving home alone myself
- Throngs of people or lines

- Enclosed areas, like theaters, escalators, or tiny shops
- Open areas like parking lots, bridges, or shopping centers
- Utilising a bus, aircraft, or another kind of public transit.
- Stressful or traumatic situations, such as the death of a parent or being attacked, may act as a trigger for the disorder, which frequently runs in families. Agoraphobics frequently, but not always, also experience social anxiety because they are afraid of having a panic attack or looking upset in front of others. They stay in the comfort of their haven, which is often their house, and avoid these places the majority of the time.
- Macrophobia, a symptom of agoraphobia, is the fear of waiting outside for extended periods.
- Agoraphobics who travel to locations where they worry they could lose control, find it difficult to get help, or risk embarrassment may have acute panic episodes.

# 6.Agyrophobia-Fear of crossing roads

The fear of crossing roads, also known as dromophobia and agyrophobia is a specific phobia that affects an individual's ability to cross a road or street where vehicles or vehicles may be present. The term "dromophobia" comes from the Greek dromos, meaning "circuit."

**Psychological signs include:**

- Being on the street
- watching a street on television.
- Observing a person cross the street

**Causes**

- ✓ As a response to a circumstance suggestive of the past horrendous event.
- ✓ Fear of going across roads may likewise result from an expectant tension connected with an individual's restricted portability.
- ✓ Dromophobia may exist in people, particularly children, who have a mental imbalance or other neurological conditions that impair their ability to judge the speed of an approaching vehicle.

# 7.Aichmophobia -Fear os sharp objects - knife

An extreme fear of sharp items is called aichmophobia. This kind of anxiety condition exists.

When around sharp instruments like

- Scissors.
- Knives.
- Needles.
- Sharp pencils.

Aichmophobic individuals suffer severe fear and anxiety. They often steer clear of circumstances or locations that feature sharp things.

As a person imagines needles penetrating their flesh while stitching, this phobia of needles may be triggered. Some individuals are afraid of anything they perceive to be sharp, ***including clothing hangers, paper clips, and umbrella tips.*** In general, more objects are viewed as triggers the worse the fear is.

The intense and irrational fear of medical treatments requiring injections or hypodermic needles is known as a "needle phobia."

# 8.Ailurophobia-Fear of Cat

Ailurophobia is the term used to describe an extreme fear of cats that is so great that it results in panic and anxiety when the cat is present or when the cat is thought about. Europhobia, gatophobia, and felinophobia are other names for this particular phobia. If you've ever had a cat bite you or scratch you, you may be wary of them. Or maybe you just don't like cats.

**Psychological signs might be:**

- Thinking about cats makes me feel nervous & afraid.
- Feeling very afraid of unfamiliar places where there could be cats.
- When you hear cats meowing, hissing, or making other similar sounds, spend a lot of time thinking about how you might meet them and how to keep them from being very scared and worried.

**Causes**

- ✓ Being jumped on or attacked by a cat.
- ✓ Encountering cats in public venues, such as the street, such as a friend's home.
- ✓ Discovering or handling cat fur.
- ✓ Having a cat lay curses on them.
- ✓ Seeing cat images in publications, online, or in books.
- ✓ Seeing or hearing cats in films or television.

# 9. Alektorophobia -fear or hate of chickens

Alektorophobia is characterised by a severe fear or haterate of chickens. Some people might become scared only by seeing a chicken or thinking about one. Although uncommon, it can also show as a dislike of foods that include chicken.

**Psychological signs:**

- Avoiding seeing or hearing about hens.
- Comprehending that fear of chickens is unjustified.
- Guilt, regret, or self-blame for having a chicken phobia.
- Still unable to manage or get over a phobia of chickens.
- Fear or panic at the mere mention or sight of chickens.
- The overwhelming desire to let a chicken alone.

**Causes**

✓ Negative encounter. An animal-related phobias are the result of a bad encounter with the animal.

✓ For instance, you could have forgotten about the violent chicken you experienced as a small child.

✓ The environment and genetics.

# 10. Anatidaephobia-Fear of ducks

Anatidaephobia is a phobia that describes the fear of being noticed by a duck, duck, or goose anywhere.

**Psychological Signs:**

- The worry that a duck may be observing you at any moment,
- Usually, their fear has gotten so bad that even watching TV shows with animals that look like ducks can make them feel terrible.

**Causes**

- ✓ They had no control over their surroundings or what happened to them. When the person encounters waterfowl in maturity, this feeling of helplessness persists.
- ✓ If a child was holding a duck and it suddenly bit
- ✓ This syndrome can happen if a child was mistreated as a child by someone who didn't like the child being around birds in general. This could lead to a lifelong fear of birds.

# 11. Algophobia - Fear of Pain

Algophobia is an extreme fear of pain in the body.

**Psychological Signs :**

- While nobody likes to be in pain, many who have this phobia experience severe fear, panic, or depressive thoughts when they think about pain.
- Additionally, algophobia's worry might increase your pain threshold. People with chronic pain disorders are more likely to experience it.
- Algophobia is the term for a fear of excessive pain. As they worry that their pain could become worse or come back, it is frequently evident in those with chronic pain syndromes.

**Causes :**

- ✓ They avoid activities or situations that they think could cause more pain or make their pain worse.
- ✓ Avoid activities or situations that you think could cause pain.
- ✓ Develop excessive fear or anxiety at the thought of pain.
- ✓ Experience a fear of pain for 6 months or longer.
- ✓ Have a reduced quality of life due to your fear of pain

# 12. Ancraophobia

Ancraophobia or anemophobia is a strong dislike of wind or draughts. For individuals who are afraid of it, it may result in panic attacks; they don't like going outside.

**Signs**

- Anxiety when imagining the wind
- Always avoid the wind.
- Incapable of managing their anxiety
- Stress in the muscles, trembling and sweating
- The mind shows a high regard for the threat that wind poses, leading to a fear of wind, even if wind may not be a hazard.

**Causes**

- ✓ Neurotransmitters and genes are both parts of genetics.
- ✓ A past traumatic event may serve as an environmental trigger.
- ✓ As an example, someone might have been injured in a wind-related accident when a tree fell on their car or them. Or perhaps one of their loved ones, like their parents, perished in this way.
- ✓ Furthermore, due to media coverage and news stories about the number of accidents caused by strong winds and wind storms, one may develop ancraophobia.

# 13.Androphobia-fear of men

Extreme anxiety or fear of men are symptoms of androphobia.

**Signs / Symptoms: -**

- When you see or think about men, you experience a sudden, extreme fear, anxiety, or panic.
- Knowingly avoiding men
- Difficulty going about your everyday activities because you're terrified of men's bodily responses to your anxieties, such as sweating, a quick heartbeat, chest tightness, or difficulty breathing.

**Causes: -**

- ✓ Prior terrible experiences with males, such as rape, physical assault, mental or physical abuse, neglect, or sexual harassment.
- ✓ A bully or someone in charge who is intimidating or overbearing (teacher, parent, or boss.
- ✓ Heredity and environment, including taught behaviour

# 14.Apeirophobia -The fear of Infinity or Eternal

The phobia of infinity, eternity auses discomfort and sometimes panic attacks.

**Symptoms & Signs :-**

- The fear of everlasting life or endless nothingness after death may be the root of apeirophobia.
- This is why it is frequently linked to hanatophobia (fear of dying).

**Causes:-**

- ✓ **Traumatic causes:** The idea of eternity or the infinite is typically associated with death. For instance, a child might be informed that his dead grandma is now sleeping "eternally This can have a deep effect on the psyche at an early age.
- ✓ **Learning:** Fear and phobias are frequently learned responses that people acquire from others. Children frequently pick up on their parents or movie characters' fear of a particular concept, in this case, infinity.
- ✓ **Genetics:** Genes have a significant impact on how anxiety develops. Some folks are simply more fearful by nature than others.

## 15. Aphenphosmphobia - fear of touching or being touched.

It is an extreme, debilitating fear of touch or intimacy is extreme anxiety about touched by anybody, including close relatives or friends.

**Signs / Symptoms**

- Avoids Handshakes
- Avoids hugs by going out of your way to keep your hands full
- People who you think have a romantic interest in you
- Form of physical interaction
- Develop nearly every time you are touched.
- Interfere with your day-to-day life and relationships.

**Causes**

- Family history of anxiety disorders.
- Other phobias or mental health conditions.
- Personal history of negative experiences with being touched.
- Personality type that tends to feel inhibited.

## 16.Apotemnophobia -Fear to become handicap -losing body parts

The excessive, unnatural, and unfounded fear of amputees (handicapped) or those who have suffered amputations is known as apotemnophobia.

An amputee (see handicap) is someone who has lost an arm or a leg due to surgery, accident, birth, or other causes.

**Signs**

- Excessive fear while approaching someone who has had a limb removed.
- Excessive fear when considering those who are handicapped.
- Unable to control anxiety
- Complete panic attacks
- avoiding physically disabled people.

**Cause**

✓ Both a person's environment and genetics may have a major impact on this illness.

## 17. Aquaphobia – Fear of Water

A fear of water is called aquaphobia. They could be scared of drinking water, swimming pools, hot baths or showers, or vast bodies of water. A traumatic childhood experience, such as a near-drowning, is a common cause of aquaphobia.**Rofiza Aboo Bakar's "Signs and Symptoms and Ways to Overcome It for Future Well-Being"** There are five typical reasons for aquaphobia:

- Drowning is an irrational fear.
- Horror event.
- Overprotective parent or parent with aquaphobia.
- Psychological problem adapting to water.
- A lack of faith in the water.

**Causes:**

- ✓ An unpleasant experience is the most typical cause of aquaphobia.
- ✓ Drowning, being in a shipwreck, or even having a poor swimming lesson.
- ✓ Many kids think that learning to swim is a rite of passage, but they often have scary experiences while doing it. Depending on how these situations are dealt with, it is very likely that a phobia will develop.

# 18.Arachnophobia -Fear of Spiders

The irrational fear of spiders and other arachnids, such as scorpions, gives rise to the particular phobia known as arachnophobia. Anyone suffering from arachnophobia will frequently feel anxious in any location where there are webs or other obvious spider presence.

**Signs & Symptoms**

- Arachnophobes who notice a spider can avoid the area until they recover from the panic episode that is frequently linked to their fear.
- When individuals come into contact with an area near spiders or their webs, some people yell, weep, have emotional outbursts, have problems breathing, sweat, and suffer higher pulse rates. In particularly severe instances, even a representation of a spider in a toy or drawing might cause tremendous fear.

**Causes**

- ✓ I had a scary spider encounter in the past.
- ✓ Exposure to a parent's arachnophobia as a child. If you experienced one of your parents' fears of spiders, you can develop arachnophobia.
- ✓ Worry or fear is related to a particular circumstance or thing, in this case, spiders.
- ✓ Immediate panic and fear make you think of a spider.
- ✓ As the spider approaches, you feel extremely threatened.Stay away from spiders.

# 19. Astraphobia -Fear of Thunder & lightening.

Astraphobia is a fear of thunder and lightning that goes too far or a fear of isolated thunderstorms that doesn't make sense. This is a sort of particular phobia; both people and animals can develop this curable fear. To feel safer, kids may seek safety and hide beneath a bed, under the covers, in a closet, in a cellar, or in some other location. The person may cover their ears or draw the curtains over the windows to muffle the thunder.

**Signs & Symptoms**

Even if they know there is no danger to them, someone who suffers from astraphobia will frequently feel nervous during a thunderstorm. Some symptoms include those common to many phobias, such as shaking, sobbing, sweating, terrified reactions, a sudden want to use the restroom, nausea, a sense of fear, putting one's fingers in one's ears, and a fast heartbeat.

**Causes:**

A particularly keen interest in weather predictions is a frequent indicator of astraphobia. An agoraphobic individual could be on the lookout for reports of impending storms. During periods of rain, they would obsessively follow the weather on television and even monitor thunderstorms online.

# 20.Atelophobia -Fear of Imperfection

Atelobophobia is an excessive and obsessive intolerance/fear of imperfections. This problem makes a person fearful of making mistakes. They typically steer well clear of circumstances where they believe they won't succeed. Atelophobia may cause anxiety, despair, and a low sense of self-worth.

**Signs / Symptoms: -**

- It is a severe form of perfectionism that can lead to low self-esteem, worry, tension, feelings of not being good enough, and hopelessness.
- People with atelosphobia frequently reinforce their fear of not being good enough through repeated self-judgment and negative self-evaluation.
- Atelophobics may also have cognitive symptoms like being unable to focus on anything but their fear, emotional isolation from others, low self-esteem, a need for constant reassurance, extreme disappointment over small mistakes, a pessimistic view of life, a tendency to set unrealistic standards for themselves, and a strong sensitivity to criticism.
- These feelings and mental states frequently result in physical symptoms such as sweating, rapid breathing, an elevated heart rate, and a parched mouth. Additional side effects include

agitation, changes in appetite, and difficulty sleeping.

- Atelophobia is a type of phobia that is caused by a fear of flaws and can lead to several mental health problems. Atelophobes often have too high of expectations for themselves and can't handle failure well. This makes them avoid certain situations and adds to their anxiety about not meeting expectations. Atelophobia may also include a variety of emotional, mental, and physical symptoms that manifest in response to specific triggering events.

**Causes:**

- ✓ Experiencing a painful event, such as receiving harsh punishment or torture for making a mistake.
- ✓ have a history of phobias, anxiety disorders, or other mental illnesses in your family.
- ✓ have additional phobias or anxiety issues.
- ✓ If you grew up in that kind of environment, you learned to strive for perfection, that mistakes were unacceptable, and that nothing you accomplished was ever good enough.

## 21.Autophobia, or a fear of being alone or Isolation.

Autophobia, also known as monophobia, isolophobia, or eremophobia, is a type of isolation phobia. It is characterised by a pathological fear of egotism or a fear of being alone.

To have the disorder, you don't have to be physically alone. You just have to feel unappreciated or ignored. The name "autophobia" doesn't mean "fear of oneself" or "fear of cars," even though "auto" is often used as a short form for "automobile" in many cultures. As with other anxiety disorders, it frequently results from and is linked to them.

In general, autophobia is seen as part of the agoraphobic cluster. This means that it has many of the same symptoms as other phobias, such as agoraphobia, with which it can be linked or paired.

**Causes:**

- Having felt abandoned as a child because of things like a parent's divorce or a death in the family, among other things, it was hard to feel alone during a painful event.
- having a parent or sibling with a different phobia than you

## Symptoms and signs

The signs of autophobia differ from case to case. However, many individuals with this condition exhibit certain symptoms. One of the most obvious signs that someone is autophobic is when they experience extreme anxiety and fear when they are alone or think about being alone. When left alone, people with this disease frequently think that a catastrophe is just around the corner. Autophobes go to great lengths to avoid being alone because of this. Even when they are not physically alone, people suffering from this illness frequently feel abandoned. In a crowded place or with a large gathering of people, autophobes frequently feel threatened.

- Not moving when alone
- Sweating
- Shaking
- Nausea
- Cold and hot flashes
- Numbness or tingling feelings
- Dry mouth
- Raising the heart rate
- Lightheadedness, dizziness

# 22. Bacteriophobia / Mysophobia - Fear of Bacteria

Mysophobia is a pathological fear of contamination and germs. It is also referred to as verminophobia, germophobia, germaphobia, bacillophobia, and bacteriophobia.Compulsive hand washing has long been linked to mysophobia. Names that closely relate to an extreme phobia of grime and mud.

**Cause: -**

- The fear of bacteria and microorganisms in general is referred to by the words "bacillophobia" and bacteriophobia.

**Symptoms and signs**

- ✓ Extensive hand-washing, avoiding areas with a high likelihood of germs, avoiding physical contact, especially with strangers, spending an excessive amount of time cleaning and sanitising one's environment, refusing to share personal belongings, and a fear of being sick
- ✓ Mysophobia has a big effect on people's daily lives and can cause symptoms as bad as trouble breathing, heavy sweating, a fast heartbeat, and feelings of panic when people are in places with a lot of germs.

# 23. Basophobia-Fear of fall & fear of walk.

Inability to walk or stand erect, due to emotional causes. The fear of falling (FOF), also known as basophobia (or basiphobia), is a normal fear that affects the majority of humans and animals, albeit to varied degrees.

**Symptoms**

- As with any other phobia, the level of fear affects how bad the symptoms are for each person.
- Debilitating anxiety, a sense of foreboding, and symptoms that are closely related to those of a panic attack, such as fast breathing, shortness of breath, sweating, an irregular pulse, a dry mouth, nausea, and the inability to express sentiments, are the main features of the disorder.

**Causes**

- ✓ Previous fall experience.
- ✓ The muscular units used for walking will become stiffer.
- ✓ Those who experience physical limitations (by accident, surgery, or pathology). may be more likely to acquire this phobia.
- ✓ The danger of basophobia might increase when older people are hospitalized.

# 24. Batrachophobia-Fear of Frogs

Fear of frogs and toads is a common superstition in many cultures. It is also the name of a specific phobia called ranidaphobia, named after the most common family of frogs. Instead of using a specific word, psychiatric specialty literature simply refers to the fear of frogs.

**Symptoms**

- Avoiding frogs and toads in both fiction and reality.
- Refusing to visit ponds, lakes, parks, or woodland regions.
- Avoiding social or educational events that might involve frogs and toads, like science classes and field trips.

**Causes**

- ✓ Genetics: An individual may come from a family with a history of anxiety and certain phobias.
- ✓ Superstitions and cultural connotations contain myths.
- ✓ If someone has a bad experience with a frog or toad, they may be afraid of them for the rest of their lives. For instance, if a small child is scared by a frog that jumps at them, the child can develop long-term phobias of frogs.

# 25. Belonephobia / Aichmophobia - Fear of needles Sharp things

The distressing fear of sharp objects—such as triangles, stars, squares, pencils, needles, knives, darts, prickly plants (such as thistles and related weeds), cactus trees, pine needles, broken glass, broken porcelain, sharp pieces of wood, a pointing finger, hexagons, or even the sharp end of an umbrella—is a type of specific phobia.

**Psychological Signs / Symptoms**

One sign of puncture phobia is a rise in heart rate and blood pressure, which is then followed by a drop in both.

- The more specific phrase known as "needle phobia" or "fear of needles" is occasionally used to describe this broad condition (trypanophobia).
- An extreme and unreasonable aversion to having an injection or using a hypodermic needle during a treatment is known as needle phobia.

**Causes**

- ✓ Many people who are afraid of needles have a close relative who also has the fear.
- ✓ Past bad encounters with needles (your own or others') also contribute to this fear.

# 26. Bibliophobia -Fear of Books

Bibliophobia is a fear of books. This anxiety frequently results from concern over the impact books may have on culture or society.

**Signs and Symptoms**

- Avoid books and locations like libraries, bookstores, and schools where they might come across books.
- Feel guilty or embarrassed about your fear.
- Get tense even just thinking about books.
- Panic when forced to handle or read a book.
- Avoid reading for personal, professional, or educational purposes.
- Excessive worry about the potential need to read or be around books

**Causes**

- ✓ Bibliophobia is a severe aversion to reading or books. This kind of anxiety condition exists. It's tough to avoid books because they are virtually everywhere.
- ✓ Bibliophobia can impair daily functioning, produce physical symptoms, and harm academic and professional achievement. Treatments include cognitive-behavioral therapy, exposure therapy, and others that may be helpful.

# 27. Blood-injection-injury (BII) -Fear of Blood

An extreme, irrational fear response to the sight of blood, an injury, or an injection, or the expectation of an injection, an injury, or exposure to blood is referred to as a "blood-injection-injury (BII)" type phobia. Pain and ketchup, which both resemble blood, can also trigger an allergic response.

**Signs & Symptoms**

- How long have you been averse to needles?
- What signs and symptoms do you get when you see a needle?
- The duration of your symptoms.
- If being afraid of needles prevents you from receiving medical care.

**Causes**

- ✓ Major hematomas can develop the following more serious injuries. Observably significant bleeding under the skin or inside bodily cavities might result from falling from a height or being involved in a car accident (chest or abdomen).
- ✓ The most common cause of hematomas is blood vessel damage or trauma. Any blood vessel damage that compromises the integrity of the blood vessel wall may result in this.

## 28. Cacophobia -Fear, Unattractiveness Aschimophobia is the fear of ugly things.

Cacophobia is a strong fear of ugly things. People who suffer from this anxiety disorder might worry about looking ugly.

**Signs & Symptoms**

- Feeling uneasy when thinking about or being close to anything unpleasant.
- Inability to handle extreme emotions.
- A highly negative self-perception.

**Causes:**

- ✓ They stay away from places and scenarios where they might run into ugly people.
- ✓ Spending a lot of time and money on cosmetic procedures and other treatments to look beautiful.
- ✓ Taking their time getting dressed or attempting to seem better.

# 29.Carcinophobia-Fear of Cancer

A typical phobia and anxiety condition, cancer phobia, sometimes called carcinophobia, is defined by a persistent fear of getting cancer. It may show up as very depressing, frightened, anxious, or distressed emotions. In certain instances, the fear may be so severe that it keeps the sufferer from leading a regular life.

**Signs & Symptoms**

- Those who have carcinophobia usually experience sadness.
- It is possible for sufferers to withdraw and develop health obsessions.
- They can get too stressed to do their normal duties.
- The fear is linked to a lack of preparation for the future and a general decline in quality of life.

**Causes**

- ✓ Cancer survivors can also develop a crippling fear of getting cancer again because of what they went through before.

# 30. Catoptrophobia / Spectrophobia - Fear of mirror

They can worry about something scary appearing in the mirror or seeing something unsettling there when they gaze squarely in the mirror and see their own image.

Some people are also afraid of their own reflections in the dark because they might look suspiciously distorted or because they could scare them.

**Signs & Causes:**

- To deliberately avoid mirrors, you could
- removing the mirrors from your home
- Not purchasing things with mirrors, such as makeup sets.
- Giving up driving because you don't like using the safety mirrors.
- Avoid going out in public for fear of seeing a mirror.

**Causes**

- ✓ People might think that mirrors are scary, dangerous, or evil because of the bad myths and ideas that have grown up around them.
- ✓ Catoptrophobia may eventually result from this.

# 31.Chemophobia-Fear on Chemicals

Chemophobia (also known as chemophobia, chemonoia, or chemophobia) is a dislike of or bias against chemicals or chemistry.

- The phenomenon has been attributed to both a rational worry about the potential negative effects of synthetic chemicals.
- An irrational fear of these substances due to misconceptions about their potential for harm, particularly the possibility that specific exposures to some synthetic chemicals may increase a person's risk of cancer.

## 32.Cherophobia (fear of happiness)

People who suffer from chemophobia think that becoming joyful would bring bad things into their lives. A person who suffers from chemophobia has an illogical fear of being joyful.

People purposefully avoid situations that elicit happiness or pleasant feelings.

**Signs / Symptoms**

- Tension while contemplating social gatherings has increased (parties, concerts, etc.).
- Rejecting opportunities to transform negative thoughts into positive ones.
- Avoiding engaging in happy or joyable events The notion that experiencing happiness will lead to unintended bad events.
- Believing that happiness is a waste of time

**Causes**

- ✓ An event from the past, preferably from childhood.
- ✓ Too much happiness "invites bad luck."
- ✓ Previous panic attacks may occur when they are happy.
- ✓ Overly stressed

# 33.Chiroptophobia-fear of bats

Chiroptophobia, or the huge fear of bats, has a similar 'flavour' of things 'swarming' around a person's head.

**Signs / Symptoms:**

Someone with this condition may find it extremely difficult to go out at night or to go into more wooded areas in an attempt to reduce the risk of coming into contact with a bat.

**Causes: -**

- ✓ Chiroptophobia is usually linked to pictures from the media, particularly how bats are represented in horror films, which may have led to vivid imaginations of bats that resulted in the fear since most people don't meet bats very often.
- ✓ as well as by early learning about danger and possible threats.
- ✓ The vast majority eat insects and fruits, and in some cases, small vertebrates.
- ✓ previous negative experiences with the phobic stimulus (in this case, bats). These experiences may have

# 34.Chromophobia -fear of colours

Chromophobia is a severe dislike fear towards colours. Most sufferers of this condition have a strong aversion to one or two specific colours, or they may just be afraid of bright colours. When a person who suffers from chromophobia sees a colour they are scared of, they experience intense anxiety or panic attacks.

**Signs / Symptoms: -**

An incident in childhood may leave a phobic with indelible emotional trauma connected to specific hues or tints that they will never be able to overcome. Numerous incidences may be connected to a certain colour, sending the phobic into a state of terror. Examples include child abuse, rape, fatalities, mishaps, and violence.

**Causes: -**

Colour phobia is also influenced by cultural roots. Certain cultures give various colours special connotations, which might be harmful for those with phobias.

# 35.Chronophobia-fear of time and time moving forward

A severe fear of time or the passage of time is called chronophobia.

**Signs & Symptoms**

- When a person with this anxiety disorder thinks about how quickly time is going by, they feel a lot of pain or fear. They could be worried about becoming older or about their own mortality. Some people become obsessed with the time or with crossing off days on a calendar.
- Because it is impossible to stop time from passing, chronophobia is particularly problematic. This illness frequently makes its sufferers feel out of control.

**Causes: -**

- ✓ Sick or old
- ✓ Witnessing a natural disaster, a near-death experience, or other horrific incident
- ✓ Prisoner's attituded
- ✓ Student during their study course tenure.

# 36.Chronomentrophobia -fear of clock & watches ticking sound.

The irrational phobia of clocks is known as chronomentrophobia.

**Sign / Symptoms:**

- anxiety if one thinks watches and clocks
- Clocks should be avoided at all costs.
- unequipped to manage their stress.
- tense muscles, shaking, and perspiration.
- may go through panic episodes.

**Causes:**

- ✓ When a person with this illness thinks about clocks, let alone actually experiences one, they might anticipate feeling an extremely high level of anxiety.
- ✓ For instance, a person with this disease could avoid going places where clocks are visible, like many companies. One of the main reasons for their mental pain is probably that they worry too much and think too much.

# 37.Cibophobia -the fear of food

The term "cibophobia" refers to a fear of eating. Ciboph obia is the fear of eating something that makes you feel stressed or panicked. There are a number of effective therapy options available if you think you or a loved one suffers from cibophobia. These can reduce or eliminate symptoms, and include cognitive behavioural therapy and hypnotherapy.

**Signs / Symptoms:**

- Dislike foods that spoil quickly.
- Fear of undercooked or overdone food
- Unsatisfied with the texture of certain foods, such as slimy or spongey, chicken with cottage cheese
- Concerns about dryness or burned edges
- Fears about eating raw food
- Fear of leftovers
- The concern that food will spoil
- Self-preparing food

**Causes**

✓ A person may develop a fear as early as infancy. When a child is exposed to someone who is terrified of particular foods, they may develop a fear themselves.

- ✓ People may avoid unhealthy meals that aren't cooked enough out of fear of getting sick from them.
- ✓ This implies that a person might not enjoy the dish.

## 38.Claustrophobia (Fear of enclosed spaces)

Claustrophobia is an anxiety disorder that causes an intense fear of enclosed spaces.

**Signs / Symptoms**

- If you get very nervous or upset when you're in a narrow place, like an elevator or overcrowded room, you might experience claustrophobia.
- Common triggers include: Small cars.
- MRI imaging machine.
- Small rooms without windows or with windows that can't be opened.

**Causes**

- ✓ A painful experience as a child
- ✓ After you were a child, you might have experienced a triggering event, like getting stuck in an elevator or flying through very rough weather.
- ✓ Childhood exposure to a parent's claustrophobia

## 39.Coimetrophobia- fear of cemeteries

Coimetrophobia is the term used to describe an unusual and lasting fear of cemeteries.

**Signs / Symptoms**:

The term "cemetery phobia" refers to those who have a negative physical and psychological reaction when they visit cemeteries rather than just dislike them. Breathing difficulties are one of the signs of this Coimetrophobia.

**Causes:**

- ✓ Like most phobias, coimetrophobia is susceptible to environmental and genetic factors.
- ✓ Cemeteries are particularly unfavorable places because death is considered taboo and bad in Western societies.
- ✓ Coimetrophobia can come from a mix of fears of the unknown, myths about cemeteries, and urban legends about places like cemeteries. The dread of being buried alive and this phobia appear to share many similarities.
- ✓ having witnessed a horror film as a child or having had a bad experience when attending a funeral

# 40.Coprophobia -fear of faces or defecation

Coprophobia is an intense dislike or fear of faces or defecation. It causes one to become afraid of their faces. When a person has this disease, even the thought of excrement might cause them to become extremely anxious, much less see it.

**Signs / Symptoms**

- Worry while expecting the face
- Incapable of managing their stress/emotions.
- Tightness in the muscles, shaking and sweating
- Possibly liable to panic attacks
- Excessive anxiety after being around excrement
- Excessive worry when considering the face
- Unable to control anxiety

**Causes:**

- ✓ Biological (genetic) and/or environmental ones (past experiences or social learning).
- ✓ For example, a person may have gotten sick or had disease after coming into contact with contaminated feces.
- ✓ One may also be afraid of faces because of the diseases they are known to carry if one is exposed to them.

# 41.Coulrophobia- Fear of clowns / jokers

Coulrophobia, the fear of clowns, maybe a crippling phobia. Clowns may cause intense, illogical emotions in children and people who are afraid of them, whether they perceive them in person or through images or recordings.

**Signs / Symptoms**

- Those who are coulrophobic typically only exhibit symptoms when they are nearby, thinking about, or witnessing clowns. Halloween
- Parties, circuses, birthday celebrations, and scary movies set a few examples of occasions that frequently set this syndrome off.

**Causes:**

✓ Frequently brought on by unpleasant memories connected to a particular situation, especially while young.

✓ If you had a terrible experience with a clown as a child, you can subsequently develop coulrophobia.

# 42. Cyberphobia-Fear of Computers & Technology.

Severe fear of computers is known as "cyberphobia". This anxiety condition can cause people to fear their cell phones and the internet. A severe case of cyberphobia may cause a person to avoid going to work, school, or any other location where there may be a computer. People with cyberphobia can control their symptoms with the aid of therapy and technical knowledge.

- Cyberphobia can manifest itself in a variety of ways. Some computer-phobic people believe they lack the skills to operate a computer, which would complicate their lives. Many people fear that a machine will ultimately replace them in their position.

- Some people are concerned that computers are recording their data and utilizing it for malicious purposes. Some people might even think computers can have a soul and turn wicked.

- Cyberphobia can sometimes be caused by bad computer experiences, like getting hacked or making a mistake that makes the computer stop working.

# 43.Cynophobia -Fear of Dogs

Cynophobia is an extreme fear of dogs. When they think about, scarcely see, or come into contact with a dog, people with this anxiety condition experience severe fear and anxiety. In extreme circumstances, this terrible fear may allegedly lead people to scarcely avoid harsh environments where dogs may be present.

**Signs of Cynophobia**

- Find unclear reasons to stay away from unknown locations or circumstances where dogs will be present.
- People frequently express their personal dislike for dogs.
- Seems agitated, tense, sweating, or trembling when there are dogs nearby.
- Attempts to dissuade concerned people from scarcely keeping dogs as abandoned pets

**Causes:**

- ✓ Traumatic events: Someone who has merely experienced a dog attack may grow afraid of dogs as a negative result.
- ✓ Family traits: Either heredity or personal environment can have an impact on the development of phobias. You are more susceptible to contracting a phobia if someone in your family does.
- ✓ Neurological conditions or physical trauma may alter how the brain functions in some sensitive

# 44.Dentophobia-fear of dentists.

Fear of the dentist is known as dental phobia. Concerned people who have with difficulty this particular phobia experience anxiety when they consider bad or go to the dentist. Dentophobia resulted from painful experiences in the past, a familial history or a sense of helplessness.

**Signs / Symptoms**

- Occur when you consider or go to the dentist.
- Prevent you from visiting a dentist, even if you're in pain or want urgent care.
- Causes anxiety or terror symptoms that by force are out of unusual proportion to the real threat.

**Causes**

- ✓ Family background
- ✓ Uncomfortable: You may find severely it odd that the dentist or hygienist is so close to your haggard face.Additionally, you could terribly worry about the critical state of your shallow breath or the wicked way your teeth appear.
- ✓ Feeling powerless: lying on the chair for an extended period of critical time with your lips opens can merely make you feel powerless.
- ✓ Past bad experiences Dentophobia can allegedly occur

## 45.Diagraphephobia-Fear of E hoarding

Diagraphebobia often referred to as "digital hoarding," "e-hoarding," "e-clutter," "data hoarding," "digital pack-rattling," or "cyber hoarding," in common is a critical condition that deals with the legitimate worry of computer files instantly disappearing.

**Fear symptoms include:**

- Concerned employees frequently take care to carefully save work .
- required to subsequently validate informed decisions since many organizations rely on email correspondence for formal approvals and decision-making.
- Since data storage devices have gotten so big and affordable, many familiar people and modern businesses don't feel the need to store data carefully.
- Active users may more easily get digital material, which can be collected faster than before, sincere thanks to the extensive availability and speedy transmission of open content on the Internet.
- Digital media willingly makes it easier for unaware people to forget how many things they have because they don't take up space and are therefore less likely to be seen as clutter. Electronic information doesn't break down or get old on its own as many physical things willingly do, so active users must carefully choose to delete it.

## 46.Domatophobia- is the fear of house or being in a house.

Domatophobia, also known as oikophobia or eicophobia, represent a fear of homes or living in homes. Mentally ill people may believe that homes are dangerous or unpleasant, especially after hearing that burglaries or even murders have occurred there in real life or culture.

**Signs / Symptoms:**

- The home may be a source of genuine fear for certain likely patients who traditionally believe in ghosts.
- This is a relatively rare fear because most individuals consider their home to remain a haven of safety and solace, a place they eagerly anticipate visiting even after travelling to more exciting or exotic locations.

**Causes:**

- ✓ The prime cause of this phobia may be claustrophobia, but it may also be the result of illogical fears such as those caused by scary movies or television shows.
- ✓ Not just young individuals vicariously experience this legitimate worry; many more elderly people grow to dislike staying home. When parents' children escape the house, there may be an emptiness in the house that causes despair. Additionally, as people age, they might not be as flexible in their movements around the house, which might act as a reminder of their death and advancing years.

# 47. Driving Phobia - Fear of Driving

The phobia of driving or riding in an automobile, also known as amaxophobia, ochophobia, motorphobia or hamaxophobia, is characterized by a persistent and strong fear of doing so.You're afraid to drive, and riding in a car with someone else can make you nervous. When someone with this illness tries to operate a motor vehicle, they immediately go into stress mode and experience symptoms like:

- ✓ Witnessing a terrible accident in the news or on social media or experiencing a car accident
- ✓ Growing up with worried parents who were time and again on the go.
- ✓ Driving under hazardous circumstances, including heavy rain, snow, or wind
- ✓ An enormous animal running in front of the automobile
- ✓ Around dangerous drivers
- ✓ There is heavy traffic.
- ✓ Traveling alone
- ✓ Fear of becoming stuck
- ✓ Afraid of accelerating
- ✓ Fearful of losing control
- ✓ Fear of death or fatalities

## 48.Dysmorphophobia - fear self-physical appearance

Body dysmorphic disorder (BDD) often still referred to as dysmorphophobia, in common is a mental illness marked by the irrational feeling that some will feel inferiority complexes about their bodies. It is a mental illness called "self" that will expose flaws in appearance.

**Symptoms:**

- Being extremely worried about something wrong with your appearance that other people can't see
- A profound conviction that you are ugly or deformed because of a physical flaw; a conviction that others notice or make fun of your appearance in a negative way.
- Excessive grooming, frequent mirror checking, or skin picking,
- Using styling, cosmetics or clothing to cover up perceived defects.
- Frequently seeking validation from people regarding your attractiveness.

**Causes:**

✓ The cause is likely complex, biopsychosocial, and the result of the interaction of several factors, like genetic, developmental, psychological, social, and cultural factors.

✓ Even though many patients mention past trauma, abuse, neglect, taunting or bullying. Develop during the early adolescent years.

## 49. Ecophobia -Fear of environmental change

Ecophobia is a moral devaluation of the environment that can cause severe environmental change.

The term "ecophobia" refers to a range of emotions that include fear, disdain, ignorance, and a lack of attentiveness toward the environment.

## 50. Eisoptrophobia-Fear of Mirrors

Eisoptrophobia, or the fear of looking in a mirror, is a type of specific phobia that doesn't happen absolutely frequently. Similar to other phobias, cognitive-behavioral psychotherapy is frequently the best treatment for this fear.

People who are afraid of being trapped could avoid having mirrors in their homes and may find it very hard to drive a car, made with many mirrors for safety. A person with eisoptrophobia will definitely feel strong spells of anxiety because of their illogical fear of mirrors, even if the severity and nature of their symptoms vary from person to person.

# 51.Emetophobia-Fear of vomiting

Emetophobia is the fear of feeling sick, vomiting, seeing someone else throw up, or seeing someone else throw up.

- While everyone occasionally gets the stomach flu, drinks too much, or gets food poisoning, some people get anxious when they actually vomit or even just think about it.

- Emotophobic people frequently have rigid diets and other self-imposed limitations, which can result in being underweight.

# 52.Enochlophobia-Fear of crowds

A fear of crowds that is illogical is called enchophobia. When in a crowd or even simply thinking about being in a crowd, a person who has this phobia feels particularly nervous.

Many people who suffer from enochlophobia make every effort to avoid large crowds.

- Movies
- Parties
- Festivals
- Amusement parks
- Shows, etc.

Agoraphobia (fear of places or circumstances) and ochlophobia (a fear of mob-like crowds) are strongly connected to it. Enochlophobia, though, is primarily concerned with the hazards you can feel among huge crowds of people.

To put it another way, someone who suffers from enoch lophobia finds it difficult to understand and manage the ir anxiety.

- Watching another person be hurt or imprisoned in a crowd).
- Being separated from your parents or becoming lost in a crowd as a young child.

- An inclination for excessive anxiety or negative thinking.
- Being nurtured by overly protective parents.
- Genetical issues.

## 53.Entomophobia-Fear of insects

An extreme or irrational fear of one or more types of insects is the defining characteristic of entomophobia, also known as insectophobia.

Fear of insects is referred to as entomophobia. When thinking about or seeing insects, a person who has entomophobia could experience intense anxiety or fear. They could also stop participating in outside activities such as walking or jogging.

## 54.Ephebiphobia-fear of youth

Ephebiphobia is the fear of children or teens; Teenagers are frequently perceived by older people as impetuous, aggressive, nasty, selfish, threatening, wild, and lazy. Teenagers may join gangs, commit crimes, and engage in acts of violence and destruction. This may increase anxiety.

Common symptoms of this phobia:

- Anxiety when thinking of ice or teenagers

- Anxiety when in the presence of teenagers
- Constantly avoiding teenagers
- Unable to cope with their anxiety
- Muscle tension, shakiness, and sweating
- May experience panic attacks.

## 55.Equinophobia-Fear of Horses

Fear of horses is known as equinophobia. This fear may be brought on by a stressful horse event, such as falling off or being kicked, trod on, or bit by a horse. You could also be terrified of horses, mules, and donkeys. You can progressively get over a phobia of horses with the use of psychotherapies like exposure therapy.

Equophobia is an unfounded aversion to horses. A person with this disease will find it very challenging to be near horses because they may worry that something horrible will occur, such as being attacked or hurt.

**Typical signs of this phobia:**

- Fear of being around horses
- Anxiety while considering horses
- Horses to avoid
- Tightness in the muscles, trembling and sweating

## 56.Ergophobia -fear of work

Ergophobia is the deep and persistent fear of work. The other names for this phobia are Ergasiophobia, or 'work aversion'. It is fear of finding or losing employment. Ergophobia is a part of social anxiety disorder. The individuals suffering from it are afraid to seek employment from fear of being yelled at by superiors, or, in general, due to performance or social anxiety.

For example, the sufferer might be afraid of performing manual labour due to the fear of getting injured.

- ✓ Ergophobia, which is not the same as being just lazy, is the fear of work or exerting a lot of "effort."
- ✓ Individuals may develop ergophobia for a variety of relational reasons, including having to accept that someone else will be "in charge" of what they do during the day (control-related concerns).
- ✓ Negative emotional experiences that are either directly or indirectly related to the thing or situational fear that causes the fear of work may be to blame.

- ✓
  With time, the symptoms frequently turn into limiting ideas in that person's life and become "normalised" and "accepted" - "I've learned to live with it."
- ✓ In many cases, as complex safety routines and behaviours have evolved, ergophobia may have gotten worse over time.
- ✓ The good news is that psychotherapy can help the vast majority of people who are afraid of going to work.

## 57.Erotophobia-fear of sexual love or sexual abuse

Excessive and unreasonable fear of sex is known as erotophobia. Those with erotophobia may be afraid of sex in multiple ways, making this illness complicated.

The following are signs that you or a loved one is afraid of a strong aversion to sexual activity

- ✓ having a great aversion to sexual stimulation
- ✓ reluctance to engage in sexual activity
- ✓ varieties of eroticism

There are several types and levels of eroticism. Some people simply despise it, while others experience great panic when trying to have a sexual relationship because of the negative connotations.

1. Genophobia or coitophobia
2. Fear of intimacy
3. Haphephobia
4. Gynophobia

**Genophobia :**

**Genophobia** also known as coitophobia, is the fear of sexual activity. Intimate connections are avoided because of the unreasonable dread of sex. Even though they may be romantically involved, they abstain from any sexual activity.

**Fear of intimacy:**

The fear of closeness is one phobia connected to genophobia. For people who are afraid of sexual closeness, it might be anything from holding hands to kissing. Deep-seated fear arises in people even when they think about sexual images or the idea of having sex.

**Haphephobia:**

This phobia is characterized by a dread of touching. The person with the condition hates being touched and avoids all physical contact. This could result in erectile dysfunction in men (ED).

**Gynophobia :** The fear of being exposed to one's bare body is known as gynophobia. Deep bodily shame and a fear of seeing others and oneself naked are potential symptoms of the illness.

**Causes Erotophobia :-**

It is more challenging to identify a purpose because there are so many different phobias associated with erotophobia. In some cases, it is impossible to pinpoint the cause of the extreme dread or panic.

- ✓ Former sexual assault
- ✓ an ingrained phobia of sexual intimacy
- ✓ skeptic of people
- ✓ Addictions
- ✓ Depression
- ✓ Suicide ideas
- ✓ Fear and worry

Genophobia or erotophobia are other names for the fear of sex or sexual intimacy. This is more than just a basic dislike or hatred. When sexual intimacy is sought, it might result in severe anxiety or panic.

- This fear either completely stops a person from being sexual or makes it very hard for them to do so.

- A specific incidence or trauma, such as sexual assault, rape, or abuse
- A learned reaction is an opinion that you picked up early in life, such as from a family member, from cultural norms, or your genes. You can be more prone to having phobias, concerns about your body or yourself, or a medical condition that makes having sex uncomfortable or unpleasant.

# 58.Genitophobia-Fear of Female

Genitophobia and eurotophobia are synonymous terms. The term "vaginaphobia," on the other hand, refers to the fear of female genitalia in the context of sexual orientation. Phallophobia is the term for the illness that has a similar male counterpart.

**Characteristics**

- Eurotophobia is sometimes a consequence of aversion to perceived by-products of female genitalia, such as discharge or mucus, which can manifest itself in both men and women and is sometimes triggered by a stressful event .
- According to the Romanian online magazine Ele, this condition being taken over by women can cause depression and self-harm, among other

things, and it comes from a very strict and prudish upbringing.

- It's possible that adult female molestation is how some people who are xenophobic developed their condition.

**Peculiarities**

Although the average individual may have an aversion to certain parts of the body, the hallmark of xenophobia is that it overcomes the reluctance displayed by most people and is a trait that can adversely affect both men and women.

The condition is sometimes linked to erotophobia and can make a person less confident in social and professional situations.

The condition can emanate both from direct antipathy and from a woman's vicarious awareness what others, such as her spouse, might think of her vulva.

**Symptoms**

- Anxiety,
- Inhibition,
- Distractions,
- Anaphrodisia and the inability to build a romantic relationship.

**Causes :-**

- ✓ The severity of the condition varies from person to person. Some people feel disgusted, while others only react when triggered. They may try to avoid thinking about female sexual organs or feel very afraid.
- ✓ Some specialists have also reported on Europhobia in the lexicon section of their publications.
- ✓ Some historical works show that Europhobic behaviour wasn't a one-time thing, but was common in some cultures. For example, couples didn't mate in well-lit areas so that the vulva wouldn't be seen.
- ✓ Some women with health problems are afraid or embarrassed to talk about their vaginas, which can make it hard to figure out what's wrong or treat it.

# 59.Erythrophobia- fear of the colour red, or fear of blushing.

The fear of getting red in the face from shyness, humiliation, or shame is known as erythrophobia.

Erythrobia is a particular phobia that results in an excessive, illogical fear of blushing. Erythrophobia is a psychological condition in which the act or concept of blushing causes extreme anxiety as well as other symptoms.

A person may avoid meeting other people or engaging in situations, such as interviews or public speaking, that may cause them to blush. Blushing occurs mainly on the cheeks and forehead, but it can also spread to the ears, neck, and upper chest. Blushing is a common physical response to feeling embarrassed or anxious.

# 60. Frigophobia-fear of becoming too cold

Frigophobia is a disorder in which a person's extremities feel cold and they have a sick fear of dying. It has been identified as a rare culturally specific psychiatric condition in Chinese communities. Only six case reports were found after a thorough literature review.

Patients would often check their hands and feet for signs of coldness before getting scared and trying to stay warm by putting on layers of clothes, using lotions, and staying close to a fire.

They stayed away from "cooling" foods and only took baths in the midday sun. Western medical assistance was sought when the intensity of the symptoms peaked or when they believed they were about to die. It is believed that the fear of dying is what motivates these people to seek assistance. Female patients were predominant, and a few of them also had concomitant-specific phobias. When necessary, short-term anxiolytic medications were used in addition to illness education, reassurance, and desensitization through exposure to cold stimuli.

# 61.Gamophobia - Fear of Marriage

If you suffer from gamophobia, or a fear of marriage or other long-term commitments, it could keep you from having happy relationships. If you had a hard breakup, or divorce, or were left by someone you loved as a child or adult, you might be hesitant to commit to someone you love. You can get over this commitment anxiety through psychotherapy.

Gamophobia is more than just being cautious or somewhat hesitant about making a big commitment. People who have this condition experience intense fear when faced with reality or even just the thought of being in a committed relationship or marriage.

Some symptoms that a person might experience include immediate feelings of anxiety, fear, or panic. It is also common for people to take steps to avoid committing an offense, such as distancing themselves from others, breaking up with the person they are dating, or avoiding dating.

There are a few reasons why someone could be afraid to get married. Here are a few common ones:

- Past failed relationships
- Children of divorce
- Apprehensions about a person

## 62. Gelotophobia-fear of being laughed at.

A person with gelotophobia might hear a stranger laugh and think it is targeted at them. In extreme cases, the reaction may include the rapid heartbeat, uncontrollable sweating, or even violence.

People have said that humour is a cure-all that makes us healthier, helps us do better at work and even makes us live longer.But other individuals find laughter to be a serious thing.

People who have gelotophobia or the fear of being laughed at, fear even jokes that are meant to be funny. They don't believe someone is just having fun when they laugh in a nice manner. Any laughing is poor laughter, according to psychologist Willibald Ruch.

# 63.Gephyrophobia -Fear of Bridges

One of the most prevalent driving phobias is the fear of bridges. Gephyrophobia remain the correct term to use. A bridge phobia can ruin your life, as everyone who has it knows. Fear can get deeper if you worry about unintentionally getting routed onto a bridge.

It's terrible to think that your only option for getting where you're going is to cross a bridge. What would normally take a 10-minute journey across a bridge to complete might take 45 minutes if drivers are desperate to avoid them. Attempting to live with a bridge phobia has this terrible side effect.

The four main phobias that can be involved include:

1. The fear of driving (Vehophobia)
2. A fear of water (Aquaphobia)
3. A fear of heights (Acrophobia)
4. The fear of being trapped (Cleithrophobia)

You may notice some other typical signs of this phobia in the list below:

- Fear while thinking about crossing a bridge
- avoiding bridge crossings at all costs.
- They struggle to manage their anxiety.
- Tightness in the muscles, trembling and sweating
- Possibly prone to panic attacks

There are four stages to overcoming a phobia of bridges.

- ✓ Reduce the sensitivity to old, unpleasant bridge-related memories.
- ✓ Determine any reactions to footage of cars travelling over bridges that can be distressing and desensitise them.
- ✓ Use cognitive therapy to deal with any bad thoughts you can't stop having about driving over bridges.
- ✓ Start exposure treatment while driving.

## 64. Genophobia -fear of sexual intercourse

Gynecophobia or coitophobia is the physical or mental fear of having sexual contact or doing sexual activities. Gynecophobia or coitophobia is the physical or mental fear of having sexual contact or doing sexual activities.Similar to panic episodes, genophobia may make people anxious and fearful. Attempts at, or even the mere concept of, sexual intercourse can have a profoundly negative impact on those who have the phobia.Relationship problems may result from overwhelming fear. Genophobic people may avoid relationships altogether to prevent the prospect of intimacy.

This could make you feel isolated. Genophobic individuals may experience loneliness as a result of feeling humiliated or embarrassed about their anxieties. Genophobia is an extreme aversion to intimate bodily actions. It is, in other words, a sex-related phobia.

## 65.Genuphobia-fear of knees or the act of kneeling

A bad encounter can sometimes, but not always, cause genuphobia. You may be more susceptible to developing this anxiety if you have already suffered a severe knee injury. The traumatic event need not, however, have occurred to you specifically. Seeing a severe knee injury happen to a friend or relative may be enough to spark anxiety. Some people have genuphobia as a result of observing a character's kneecaps break in a gangster movie.

# 66.Gerascophobia- Fear of Aging or the Fear of Dying

Those who have genuphobia, or a fear of knees, could find the appearance of knees repulsive. Or they could be concerned about the possibility of knee damage. When they see or touch knees, cross their legs or have to kneel, they may get anxious.Gerascophobia, often known as the fear of ageing or the fear of dying or developing an age-related medical condition, is the fear of growing old.

Fear of ageing or becoming older is known as gerascophobia. Fear is a negative emotion that arises in reaction to a threat, actual or imagined and involves cognitive, behavioural, and physiological components. Additionally, it may result from the displacement of an emotion brought on by another external stressor (e.g., sexual abuse).

As a result of the heightened knowledge of the negative effects of ageing on the body, more people are increasingly turning to alternative forms of treatment.The major reason why people fear getting older is because, in addition to significant health problems, they are moving closer to death.symptoms of suffering might be Repulsiveness, disgust, nausea, lack of appetite, suicidal thoughts, sadness, dizziness, difficulty thinking or speaking clearly, trembling, palpitations, and fast breathing are some symptoms that sufferers may experience. Gerascophobia can, however, also be quiet.

# 67.Gerontophobia-a hatred or dislike of senior citizens (Aged people)

An aversion or hatred towards elderly people. Gerontophobia is an aversion to or fear of the elderly caused by memento mori or the fear of old age self-degeneration (similar to gerascophobia). It is also a fear of aging.

Gerontophobia is a fear of self-degeneration that comes with getting older, similar to gerascophobia. It can also be a dislike or aversion to the elderly because of memento mori. It can also be a phobia. A dislike or hostility for senior citizens.

Gerontophobia and aging's discriminatory characteristics are closely related. This unreasonable fear or hatred of the elderly may be related to the assumption that, like all other young people, including oneself, one will eventually grow old and experience the irreversible health deterioration that comes with aging, which is linked to disability, sickness and death. Emotions of hatred and acts of prejudice against the elderly can result from this refusal to accept them.

## 68. Globophobia

A fear of balloons is known as balloon phobia or globophobia. The source of fear may be the sound of balloons popping. People who have globophobia typically don't confront, touch, or feel a balloon out of concern that it may pop. This is a kind of phonophobia.

## 69.Glossophobia-Public speaking phobia

Glossophobia is the term for a serious phobia of public speaking. It is a particular kind of phobia, an anxiety condition marked by a continuous and intense feeling. The fear of social situations, or social phobia, is a subgroup of glossophobia. Most glossophobics don't show signs of other sorts of phobias.

The fear of social circumstances, or social phobia, is a subgroup of glossophobia. Most glossophobics don't show signs of other social phobias, including a fear of meeting new people or a fear of doing things in front of others. Many people who suffer from glossophobia can perform on stage in dance or song as long as they are not required to speak. However, stage fright is a fairly common occurrence in glossophobic people.

# 70.Gymnophobia-fear of nudity

Since the beginning of time, people have disagreed about how the human body should be shown. While some see it as a person's natural state, others view a naked human body as something commonplace or obscene that shouldn't be displayed.

Gymnophobia, which is also called nudofobia, is a type of phobia that is grouped with anxiety disorders. The person who has this particular phobia suffers from a pathological fear of both their own and other people's nudity.Similarly, through case studies, it has been confirmed that a feeling of inferiority towards the body itself pervades many gymnophobic patients and that this emotion continues to be the root cause of the phobia's emergence.

Gynophobia is the term for terror or extreme fear that happens when a person's dislike of seeing someone naked goes beyond disgust or anger.Gymnophobia, or the dread of nudity, is a phobia that is unique to each individual. Some people with this fear only feel anxious when they are naked in public places like locker rooms or public showers. But some people are also afraid of exposing themselves when they are alone or with their partner. Other people also have a dread of being naked alone.

Because of their fear of gyms, many people with gymnophobia can't do sexual things and may develop a broader fear of sex as a result. In extreme situations, this phobia may even develop into a fear of taking a bath or shower. While some people don't mind being naked themselves, they find other people's nakedness unsettling.

**Causes**

Many factors can contribute to gymphobia. There is no doubt that those who have experienced sexual trauma are more likely to develop the phobia, in part because they feel more exposed when naked or because nudity triggers their anxiety.

Being brought up in a conservative society or religion that discourages sexual expression and nudity can also result in a fear of nudity (or, more popularly, a fear of sex). This anxiety can also develop in kids and young teenagers who experience bullying or embarrassment because of their bodies, such as if they are growing faster or slower than their classmates.

Two other phobias that might sometimes be linked to gymnophobia are the fear of being close and the fear of being weak. It may also be related to social anxiety, body dysmorphic disorder, and other illnesses that make people excessively harsh on themselves. And lastly, having surgery scars or other physical flaws might make someone feel worse about their bodies, which can quickly lead to a fear of gyms.

**Coping Strategies**

Little changes are often found to be effective in reducing gymnophobia in sufferers.

They might forego taking a shower after working out, or they might prefer to have sex in the dark. Other examples include refusing to buy in establishments with shared restrooms. This alone may be sufficient for people with mild to moderate gymnophobia to prevent the condition from interfering with their daily lives.

Yet with time, the anxiety can get worse, and gynophobia people would find themselves having to stop doing an ever-growing number of things to avoid baring their bodies. Gymnophobia must be addressed when it is having a severe negative impact on a person's life, such as when they stop taking a bath.

Simply learn how to stop thinking about your current fears. It will take time and work to overcome gymnophobia no matter which route you choose, but the benefits are well worth the trouble.

# 71.Gynophobia-Fear of Women

Gynophobia is the term for a fear of women. According to historians, the phrase came to be used to describe men's fear of being humiliated by women. When you overreact to a circumstance, a fear of women might develop into a phobia in the clinical sense.

When you overreact to a circumstance, a fear of women might develop into a phobia in the clinical sense.

Like other phobias, the exact cause of gynophobia is not well understood. Factors related to experience and environment have a significant impact on gynophobia. The formation of this phobia frequently involves any painful or unfavourable experience with a female. Any form of female abuse—mental, sexual, or physical—can induce fear or anxiety in people who are around women.

Previous unpleasant or unfavourable experiences with women, such as abuse, rape, sexual harassment, or physical assault, are among the signs.

# 72. Halitophobia- fear of bad breath

Halitosis is another name for bad breath. It is a condition in which the mouth has a strong, unpleasant smell.For individuals who are impacted, it may cause worry. Additionally, it has been linked to obsessive compulsive disorder symptoms and depressive symptoms.

Simply put, halitophobia is an extreme fear of having bad breath for no reason. People who suffer from halitophobia are convinced that they have terrible breath and that this is having an adverse effect on their lives. This problem could be becoming more prevalent because more attention is being paid to treatments that address foul breath.

It's common to spend a brief period of time stressing about bad breath before a significant occasion, such as a business meeting or a job interview. However, those who have halitophobia worry about their breath all the time, interfering with their regular activities.

## 73.Haphephobia - fear of being touched

An extreme, irrational fear of touching is known as haphephobia. It differs from hypersensitivity, which is physical pain caused by touch. Haphephobics experience severe anxiety at the mere notion of being touched. Physical symptoms like nausea, vomiting, or panic attacks may result from this worry.

Haphephobia can have a significant impact on your life. The harshness and nature of contact have an impact on the symptoms of this illness. Life interruptions might result from a strong sense of fear or a strong reaction.

## 74.Heptadekaphobia, -fear of the number 17

The phobia of the number 17 is known as heptadekaphobia. It is seen as unlucky in Italy and other nations with Greek and Latin roots, with the date Friday the 17th being particularly unlucky in Italy. Superstition has caused people to fear the number, which is comparable to how Anglo-Saxon nations fear the number 13.Friday the 17th, which is Italian in origin, is considered unlucky because it combines two unfavourable elements: Friday (from Good Friday, the day of Jesus' death), and the number 17.

## 75.Hedonophobia-fear of obtaining pleasure

Those who suffer from cherophobia most often aren't always depressed; instead, they avoid situations and interests that can make them happy. Some individuals fear joy and happiness.

Even though they avoid things they find fun, like social events and activities, this doesn't mean they are always sad. Among the signs of the disease are:

- When you receive an invitation to a social event, anxiety sets in.
- refusing to take part in activities that are "fun."
- believing that happiness predicts bad fortune.
- Feeling happy makes you a terrible or worse person, in your opinion.
- believing that being happy is harmful for you, your friends, or your family.
- believing that attempting to be happy is a waste of time and energy.

# 76.Heliophobia-Fear of Sun

Heliophobia is a term for a severe, occasionally illogical aversion to the sun. Some individuals who have this illness also fear bright, indoor light.

Heliophobia, like other phobias, can have a variety of causes. Some people may develop a fear of light as a result of reading material about skin cancer that makes them anxious or distressed.The extreme fear of developing skin cancer may be the root cause of heliophobia in certain people. Others could experience a profound, paralysing fear of photoaging and wrinkles.Some people may need to cover up in a lot of clothes, apply sunscreen liberally on exposed skin, and wear dark-colored eyewear before going outside.

# 77.Helminthophobia -fear of worms

Fear of having worms in one's body is known as helminthophobia. Helmintho, which means "worm," and phobia both have Greek roots (meaning fear). Vermiphobia, another name for helminthophobia, is connected to scoleciphobia (a phobia of worms), taeniophobia, and teniophobia (which both mean fear of tapeworms).

## 78.Hemophobia, haemophobia -fear of blood

Fear of blood or harm is what this is. When exposed to their own blood or that of another person. The word "hemophobia," or "blood phobia," is used in medicine to characterise an extreme and illogical fear of blood that impairs a person's ability to go about their daily life.

The psychological examination, which consists of a structured interview with a mental health expert, is the basis for the diagnosis of hemophobia. It gives information to analyse the person's behaviour, personality, thought processes, and cognitive capacities and, as a result, detect any problems.

## 79.Herpetophobia -fear/dislike of reptiles or amphibians

Fear of reptiles is known as herpetophobia. This is applicable to all reptiles, although most frequently it refers to snakes and lizards. Herpetophobia is a particular phobia, a sort of anxiety disease. When a person has a certain phobia, they are particularly nervous around that particular thing.Specific phobias are a fairly common anxiety disorder.Many individuals will probably encounter one at some point in their lives. The most prevalent reptile phobia is that of snakes.

# 80.Hexakosioihexekontahexaphobia - fear of the number 666

The intense and enduring fear of the number 666 is known as hexakosioihexekontahexaphobia. It most likely pertains to a passage from the New Testament that makes mention of the beast's number and the number 666.

There are several ways to read this text, and some of them suggest that the number represents the Antichrist or Satan. Some people avoid dates and even store receipts containing sixes because they are so afraid of the number. People might not realise the fear is unjustified since it is so tightly tied to religion.

# 81.Hippophobia -fear of horses

A psychological fear of horses is known as equinophobia or hippophobia. Even when a horse is known to be kind and well-trained, those who have this phobia endure excessive worry. Usually, they steer clear of horses completely to prevent the possibility of being bit, kicked, or thrown. They could also be afraid of mules, donkeys, and other animals with hooves.

A fall from a horse may cause this kind of anxiety, (which is probably why it is said that, after a fall from a horse, one should get right back on).

## 82. Hodophobia -fear of travel

The medical name for a severe fear of travelling is homophobia. They refer to it as "trip-a-phobia." It frequently involves a heightened fear of a certain means of transportation, like aircraft. It's a phobia that can also develop in the wake of widely reported tragedies and occurrences that frighten people.

The fear of travelling is typically brought on by a bad travel experience in the past. You experience a more intense bodily and mental stress reaction as a result of remembering the incident. For example, the thought of using the same mode of transportation as the traumatic incident would cause panic attacks and anxiety.

**Real examples:**

- You are unable to go alone. You could rely on friends or relatives to accompany you on your trip. They could make you feel better and somewhat take your mind off your anxieties.
- When you're travelling in a group, you have a terrible fear of being lost or losing touch with friends, family, or co-workers.
- You are terrified of taking any mode of transportation, whether it is a bus, a train, a ship, or an airplane.
- You can't operate a vehicle or ride in one.

- You're anxious about leaving your house. Sometimes, this is mislabeled as a social phobia or claustrophobia. However, under these circumstances, your fear is of the actual journey rather than of mingling or enclosed environments.
- You could have a panic attack when trying to plan a vacation, check your luggage, or do anything else.

**Tips to overcome**

- Avoid using drugs and alcohol.
- Learn What to Expect.Look up information about your hotel online. View the seating diagrams for your airline or train or the deck layouts for your cruise ship.
- Map out your route. If you're travelling by car, get ahead with a map and determine how much distance you'll cover each day.
- Give yourself enough time to be there early, and have a backup strategy in the event of delays.
- Rest and drink water.
- Imagine yourself taking each of your journey's main steps in your mind's eye

## 83.Hydrophobia-fear of water, see aquaphobia

Fear of the water is known as hydrophobia. People who have hydrophobia are very fearful of the image or thought of water. They could be scared of drinking water, swimming pools, hot baths or showers, or vast bodies of water.

an unreasonable fear of drinking or swimming in water. "Hydrophobic" refers to someone afraid of the water. a word that was historically frequently used to describe rabies because, in the disease's latter stages, the animal (or human) has trouble swallowing and is afraid to take a drink of water.

great fear or phobia of water, particularly when accompanied by painful, uncontrolled throat spasms brought on by rabies. In actuality, this is not true (although rabies does cause mental confusion of other kinds).

When rabies is far along, it moves from the first cut to the central nervous system, which causes a fear of water.

# 84. Hypnophobia, somniphobia -fear of sleep or nightmares

Extreme or illogical apprehension about falling asleep is known as hypnophobia.

Hypnophobia is a long-lasting, irrational fear of hypnotism or sleep that is thought to come from a person's unconscious mind.Medical data shows that an individual's emotional state leads to wakefulness in response to a perceived threat or danger that disrupts sleep patterns, even if the exact cause of hypnophobia is still mostly unclear.

While thinking about going to bed, hypnophobia causes extreme anxiety and terror.Somniphobia, clinophobia, sleep anxiety, or sleep fear are other names for this phobia.

Hypnophobia-specific mental health symptoms may include: experiencing fear and worry while thinking about sleep, delaying bedtime or staying up as late as possible, having panic attacks when it's time to sleep, and having problems falling or staying asleep.

# 85.Hypochondria -fear of illness

Disorder of illness anxiety, often known as hypochondriasis or health anxiety. It is excessively scary that you have or might get a serious illness.

You might not be physically ill. You can also think that common bodily sensations or minor symptoms indicate a major medical issue, despite the fact that a careful physical examination reveals no such thing.

Types of diseases and anxiety disorders: Those who suffer from illness-related anxiety disorders typically fall into one of the following groups:

**1.Care-seeking:**

You spend a significant amount of time in a hospital setting. You request medical testing and consult with many doctors.

**2.Care-avoidant:**

You avoid going to the doctor and receiving medical attention. You could not believe in medical professionals or believe they don't treat your symptoms seriously. More worry and fear may result from this.

**Symptoms:**

- Avoiding people or places out of concern for becoming sick.
- Constantly looking up symptoms and illnesses.
- Exaggerating the intensity of the symptoms (for instance, a cough becomes a sign of lung cancer).
- A lot of concern over one's health.
- Obsession with physiological processes like heart rate.
- Discussing excessively with people about your health and symptoms.
- Testing your temperature or blood pressure on a regular basis for disease symptoms.
- Requesting assurances regarding your symptoms or health from close friends or family.
- Discomfort from healthy bodily processes like perspiration or flatulence.
- A concern that you may develop a major illness because of minor symptoms or physical feelings.

# 86.Ichthyophobia -Fear of fish

Ichthyophobia unfounded dislike for fish or fish-related items. It is a phobia of fish, such as a phobia of eating or seeing dead fish.

It is a phobia of fish, such as a phobia of eating or seeing dead fish. When a person has this disease, even the thought of fish might cause them to become particularly nervous, let alone when they actually see one. Their worry may even be so severe that it causes them to have a full-blown panic attack.

Ichthyophobic individuals may notice themselves avoiding the things they are afraid of. By making sure they are never exposed with fishes in any form, they might take this to an extremity. To avoid seeing any fish, a person with this disease may, for instance, avoid all bodies of water. One of the primary reasons for their mental suffering is likely due to such excessive concern and unreasonable thinking.

# 87.Insectophobia-Fear of Insects

Extreme and persistent fear of insects is known as "insectophobia. It's a type of phobia known as a "specific phobia," which concentrates on a single item. One of the most prevalent forms of specialized phobia is insect fear.

An excessive phobia makes you extremely anxious. It's not the same as merely disliking them or experiencing their presence and knowing whenever one scurry by. Some people have crippling anxiety that prevents them from going about their normal lives.

Therapy tries to keep your phobia from making your life worse by teaching you how to control your reactions to insects.

## 88.Koumpounophobia -fear of buttons on clothing

The phobia of clothing buttons is referred to as koumpounophobia. When victims with this phobia are exposed to buttons physically or visually, they frequently experience sensations of anxiety and revulsion.

Instead of being actively terrified of buttons, people may actually feel repulsed by them. Researchers have proposed a strong connection between disgust and fear. You can start to avoid pressing some buttons if you find their texture repulsive. Even though a button phobia might significantly affect your everyday life, it is treatable with professional assistance and diligent effort.

## 89.Lilapsophobia

Lilapsophobia, or the fear of hurricanes, is especially prevalent among people who live in areas where a hurricane is a real possibility, such as the south and east of the United States and other parts of the world.It is disputed if this is a phobia or a valid fear, but a lot will depend on whether you have ever personally experienced a storm. Strong fear might interfere with your everyday life and get worse with time. Lilapsophobia is an unhealthful aversion to hurricanes or tornadoes. The most popular kind of treatment is for psychological stress. It may help you cope with lilapsophobia's negative effects on your daily life.

# 90.Lepidopterophobia -fear of butterflies and moths

The phobia towards butterflies or moths is known as lepidopterophobia.

Although some people could have a minor fear of such insects, phobias are when you experience an overwhelming and unreasonable fear that affects your day-to-day activities. Lepidoterophobia is more common than is known.

A fear of an insect's potential reaction, such as it leaping on you or touching you, heredity, a bad or traumatic encounter with it, or a rapid introduction to the worm, can all contribute to a fear of insects like butterflies or moths.

If left untreated, a phobia can be severe and last a lifetime. If you think your child is exhibiting symptoms of a phobia, it's a good idea to start by taking them to the doctor.

# 91.Mageiricophobia -fear of cooking

An extreme fear of cooking is called mageirocophobia. It is a specific phobia, which means that it makes a person afraid of a certain circumstance. A lot of individuals have anxiety when cooking, whether it be for themselves, others, or both.

The following actions can have an impact on your day-to-day life: refusing to enter a kitchen out of fear of witnessing someone cook; Avoiding restaurants to avoid the risk of watching other people cook and working in professions that do not require you to observe or think about people cooking

Cooking phobia, often known as mageirocophobia, has several symptoms. Others are afraid to make poached eggs for themselves, while some people are just scared of cooking for large parties. Mageirocophobia is a very noticeable phobia; however, it is not considered a phobia unless it significantly interferes with everyday living.

**Types of cooking phobia**

- **Fear of Illness Spread: Due to media attention, we assume that they occur frequently.** Those who have this phobia typically fear contamination, spoiling, and/or undercooking.

- **Fear of Serving Inedible Food:** They lack confidence in their taste buds or ability to choose the right ingredients for each meal.

- **Presentation Issues:** Some chefs strive for perfection. They could be concerned with how the food appears, if the glasses are spot-free, or even whether the tablecloth is evenly spaced.

- **Fear of the Cooking Procedure:** Many cooks are afraid of slicing themselves, getting burned, or running into other problems throughout the process. Some people are terrified of methods they do not completely comprehend, like poaching and blanching.

- **Fear of Recipes:** Some chefs are scared off by recipes that look excessively difficult or lengthy. They can fear their capacity to complete all of the stages or fear that they will miss something.

Overcoming methods

- Get the ideal recipe.
- Be receptive.
- Keep a sense of humor and a fallback strategy handy.
- Pre-cooking. Before even considering making the meal, go over everything completely from beginning to end.
- Cook collectively

# 92.Masklophobia -fear of people in masks, costumes and mascots

The phobia of individuals in masks and costumes, including mascots, fully body-covered dresses, masquerade costumes, and Halloween costumes, is known as mysophobia. Extremely many people have a fear of masks, or mask phobia, particularly kids.

Maskaphobia is a very personal condition. Some people just have a phobia of scary or ghostly masks. Some people may even experience a generalized fear that includes figures in costumes in addition to masks. Maskaphobia and clown phobia may be connected.

To be called mysophobia, your fear of masks and costumes must include the following:

- Incredibly difficult-to-control feelings of panic, worry, or terror.
- Unfounded fear or worry in the face of a threat.
- Avoidance behaviors are used to avoid coming into contact with masks or costumes.
- A fear of masks and costumes affects your daily life, general welfare, or sense of safety.
- Being confronted by a cartoon figure the size of Mickey Mouse. As most kids are trained not to talk to strangers, this fear may also be explained by the fact that they may become confused and uneasy when they come across a giant costumed character.

## 93. Megalophobia- fear of large objects

Megalophobia is an anxiety condition where a person has a severe fear of big things. When confronted with or in the vicinity of huge items such as large buildings, sculptures, animals, and automobiles, such as aeroplanes, blimps, buildings, buses, construction equipment's, elephants, massive trees, such as sequoias or redwoods, heights, and peaks, large water bodies, ships, statues, trains, whales, etc.

## 94.Melanophobia -Fear of the Colour Black or Dark Colours.

The unpleasant fear of the color black or other dark colors is known as melanophobia.

Anyone with melanophobia will experience extreme fear when they view or think of anything dark. Some people get panic attacks because of their great fear.

These emotions are frequently caused by what dark hues stand for danger, darkness, death and lamentation, despair, evil, being lost, loneliness, and night.

The behavioural symptoms are

- Avoiding black-colored objects, even if you need them. A medicine bottle with a black label, for instance.
- When going outside at night, feeling uneasy or out of control.
- Refusing to leave the house due to fear of seeing dark colors.
- Being afraid to close your eyes.

## 95.Melissophobia -fear of bees

Severe fear of bees is known as melissophobia, sometimes known as apiphobia. This fear might be paralyzing and extremely stressful.

One of many distinct phobias is melissophobia. Specific phobias are a type of anxiety disorder.
People with a specific phobia have a deep, irrational fear of an animal, object, or situation.

Psychological signs of melissophobia include feeling a sudden, intense fear or anxiety when you think about or see bees, avoiding places or situations where you might be around bees, and knowing that your fear is unfounded but you can't do anything about it.

# 96.Monophobia-fear of being alone or isolated or of one's self

The uncontrollable and unreasonable fear of being alone is known as monophobia or autophobia. Your relationships, social life, and profession may all be impacted by this fear of being alone. You can also be terrified of being abandoned because of a painful incident you had as a child.Monophobia, often known as the fear of isolation, such as the fear of:

- Being apart from a specific individual,being alone at home
- Being alone in a public place, feeling forgotten or alone,being at risk on my own
- Being single,Loneliness,Solitude

**Causes**

Hardship during infancy may also contribute to monophobia.

- Abuse
- passing of a parent
- Divorce
- Domestic abuse
- Financial issues within the family
- prolonged absence of a parent
- Neglect
- drug abuse or mental disorders in the parents
- a family member's serious sickness

Many individuals fear being alone, even in their own homes.

## 97.Musophobia/murophobia, fear/fear of mice or rats

Musophobia is an irrational and severe fear of mice and rats. When you come into contact with mice or rats, someone who has musophobia may experience acute fear, panic, or anxiety. Although many individuals will have understandable apprehensions and worries about mice and rats, those who suffer from musophobia feel an overpowering fear, worry, and panic that is out of proportion to the dangers. Although the fear of rats and mice is the main symptom of musophobia, some sufferers also have a phobia of other rodents, such as guinea pigs.

**Musophobia signs and symptoms**

- Extreme phobia of mice or other rodents stresses while considering mice or other rodents.
- Viewing a picture of mice or other rodents might make you feel overwhelmed.
- Shivering and fainting when they see a rat or mouse.
- While being aware that your feelings of fear, worry, or anxiety are extreme, being unable to control them.
- A desire to escape or hide.
- Feeling trapped or unable to escape.
- A phobia of death or dying.
- Having trouble carrying out everyday tasks while among mice or rats.

# 98.Mycophobia- dislike to mushrooms

Mycophobia is an unreasonable fear of all fungi, such as mould, toadstools, and mushrooms. The unreasonable fear of mushrooms is known as mycophobia. A person with this syndrome might anticipate feeling extremely anxious just by thinking about mushrooms. Their worry may even be so severe that it causes them to have a full-blown panic attack. Although not everyone with mycophobia may experience such a surge in anxiety, it can happen. tightened muscles, shaking, and profuse perspiration, among other symptoms.

**Signs and symptoms**

- Several more signs of this phobia include:
- When considering mushrooms, you feel anxious.
- avoiding mushrooms all the time.
- Unable to manage their anxieties
- Anxiety, trembling, and perspiration in the muscles
- possible panic attacks

# 99.Myrmecophobia -fear of ants

The illogical fear of ants is known as myrmecophobia. Due to their great fear of coming into contact with ants, people with this mental condition may find it exceedingly difficult to go for walks on trails or to be outside in strange places.

**Myrmecophobia has the following causes or symptoms:**

People who are afraid of ants, called myrmecophobes, may decide to live in a city instead of a more rural area with the land because they are afraid of ants. If a person with myrmecophobia lives on a big piece of land, they might go to a lot of trouble to spray pesticides on their lawn and might worry too much about it.

It's crucial to determine whether someone with myrmecophobia also has an obsessive-compulsive disorder.

# 100. Mysophobia-Fear of germs & dirt

A severe fear of germs & dirtiness is known as mysophobia. You could go out of your way to stay away from situations where you could be exposed to germs. The phobia gets worse with time, as do your precautions. Similar to obsessive-compulsive disorder, you could become caught in a loop of repetitive activities that negatively impact your quality of life (OCD).

**Sign & Symptoms**

- Avoiding areas that are believed to be filled with a lot of filth or bacteria
- Extreme dislike of becoming sick
- A lot of hand washing
- A concern for cleanliness
- Overusing sanitizing or cleaning supplies

**Causes:**

- ✓ Avoid going to events that are required of you, such as meetings and holiday festivities.
- ✓ Having anxiety, sadness, or other phobias runs in the family.
- ✓ enduring a horrific incident that makes one unduly preoccupied with filth, pollution, or germs
- ✓ Obsessive-compulsive disorder (OCD)

# 101.Necrophobia-fear of death or the dead

Necrophobia is an irrational fear of dead objects and things associated with death, such as corpses (e.g., coffins, tombstones, funerals, emeteries).Obsession with death manifests itself in both curiosity and objectification of all types of emotion.Necrophobia can also refer to a cultural fear of the dead, such as the conviction that the deceased's ghosts will come back to torment the living.

The patient could feel this way constantly or just when a frightful event, such as seeing a dead animal up close or attending a funeral, sets off the terror.

**Causes: -**

- A traumatic event in the past—The phobic may have seen the death of a close relative when they were young, which eventually led to their great fear of death.
- Learned reaction: Many phobias and worries are in fact absorbed from the environment. A young child could, for instance, see an adult they trust reacting in fear. Then he or she chooses a related response.

- Overly stressed parents run the risk of instilling the same mentality in their children.
- The terrified reaction one has to everything associated with corpses or dead objects can be pretty humiliating. This creates a vicious loop since the person keeps repeating these bad feelings and ideas out of fear of getting the wrong answer. This makes her or him even more terrified of coming upon a circumstance involving corpses.
- Chronic, unresolved stress can also lead to phobias. If anxiety, sadness, or stress at work or in one's personal life are not controlled, they may turn into phobias.
- Media such as movies, books, and television can contribute to the feeding of phobias.
- Genes: A lot of phobias, including necropsia, are inherited. Some people are predisposed to certain anxiety disorders more than others due to certain genes.

## 102.Neophobia -fear of newness, novelty, change or progress

The fear of the unfamiliar or new is known as neophobia.The fear could be largely related to particular things, such as a fear of trying new foods or going to new places. Limiting a person's life, relationships, and experiences can also have a major negative impact. Neophobia, or the fear of the strange, contradicts humans' need for novelty. It could not even be identified as a fear in its mildest manifestations.

**Signs:**

- Excessive and unwarranted fear in the presence of new changes.
- A quick reaction of fear when faced with new situations.
- Avoiding new adventures or suffering serious discomfort when exposed to them.

**Causes**

- ✓ Traumatic or upsetting situations may also be important.
- ✓ Neophobia may be linked to the dual fears of failure and success.
- ✓ Example people typically reside in the same home for many years, work for the same company, drive the same vehicle, and even eat the same meal.

# 103.Nyctophobia -Fear of Darkness / Night

Nyctophobia is a severe phobia of the night or the dark that can have severe depressive and anxiety symptoms. When a fear becomes overwhelming, unreasonable, or negatively affects your daily life, it is called a "phobia."

The fear of the dark frequently begins in childhood and is seen as a typical stage of growth. Studies about this phobia have shown that people often have a fear of the dark because they can't see anything.In other words, because they are unable to see their surroundings, people may be afraid of the dark and the night.

**Signs / symptoms**

- Being nervous in any darkly lit setting
- Being hesitant to leave the house at night
- Being compelled to spend time in the dark, experiencing physiological symptoms such as an elevated heart rate, perspiration, obvious shaking, and even feeling sick.
- Need a nightlight to sleep
- Trying to get away from dark areas.
- When someone attempts to get you to spend time in the dark, becoming aggressive or defensive
- Compulsion to spend the night inside

- Intense feelings, screams in the dark, and tears.

**Causes**

- ✓ Nyctophobia, also known as scotophobia, achluophobia, and lygophobia, is a fear of needles.
- ✓ The fear could not be caused by the darkness itself, but rather by the threats that hide there (which is why horror and suspense movies often use darkness as a way to scare viewers).
- ✓ Lack of safety / security, and trust can also contribute to this, particularly if you experience night-time phobia more frequently while you're by yourself.
- ✓ Some psychoanalytic writers think that separation anxiety from a key attachment figure may be connected to a person's fear of the dark.
- ✓ entering a darkly lit area (like a movie theatre).
- ✓ Preparing for bed.
- ✓ Observing the sun set.
- ✓ Imagining being in the dark
- ✓ Trying to get some sleep at night.
- ✓ Closing the lights.
- ✓ Watching a film or television programme featuring sequences set at night.

# 104.Nomophobia -fear of being out of mobile phone contact

Nomophobia is an abbreviated form of "**no**-**mo**bile-**pho**ne pho**bia**." Nomophobia is a series of psychological symptoms in which a person worries or is nervous about not having access to a mobile phone. While some people may not enjoy the notion of living without their phones for an extended period, others may feel panic or anxiety when their mobile phone loses connectivity. Nomophobia is the term for this.

**Signs / Symptoms**

- You are unable to turn off your phone.
- Scanning your phone constantly for missed calls, emails, or texts
- Even when your phone is almost fully charged, charging your battery
- Carrying your phone everywhere you go, including the restroom
- Confirming that you have your phone regularly
- Apprehension over being unable to access a cellular data network or WIFI
- Worrying about unfavorable events occurring and being unable to seek assistance
- Stress associated with losing one's online identity or presence

- Skipping planned activities or events in favor of using a mobile device
- Without continual access to information via my smartphone, I feel uneasy.
- Would be scared if my smartphone's battery died.

**Causes**

- ✓ Smartphones are capable of a wide range of tasks. People use their phones to communicate, do business, remain organized, exchange personal information, and even manage their finances.

- ✓ People worry about losing their phones because they use them for so many important things. People who are without their phones may feel cut off from crucial facets of their lives, such as friends, family, their job, finances, and information.

# 105.Nosocomephobia -fear of hospitals

Hospitals cause a strong, excessive fear known as nosocomephobia. When visiting a hospital or merely thinking about one, those who have a phobia of them feel extreme worry and discomfort. In order to avoid clinical environments and medical care, they could go to tremendous lengths, which could be dangerous for their health and safety.

**Signs / Symptoms**

- Fear of enclosed spaces.
- Fear of blood.
- Fear of doctors.
- Fear of germs.
- Fear of death
- Fear of needles

**Causes**

- ✓ A person who suffers from nosocomephobia can typically refuse to go into a hospital, even if their illness is life-threatening.
- ✓ In addition, even knowing that their fear is unfounded, they will nevertheless feel helpless in the face of it.

## 106.Nosophobia-fear of contracting a disease

Nosophobia is the persistent, illogical fear of developing a chronic, frequently fatal illness, such as cancer or AIDS, COVID-IX. The disease anxiety condition (hypochondria) that causes you to be concerned about all illnesses is not the same as nosophobia.Sometimes the name for this particular phobia is just "disease phobia."

**Nosophobia symptoms include:**

- Reducing your chance of contracting an illness by avoiding certain people or locations.
- Continually investigating a particular illness and its signs.
- Extreme concern for your well-being.
- Fearing that a cough is an indication of lung cancer or obsessing about physiological processes like heart rate.
- Discussing excessively with people about your health and symptoms.
- Testing your temperature or blood pressure on a regular basis for disease symptoms.

- Requesting assurances regarding your symptoms or health from others.
- Discomfort with regular body processes like flatulence or perspiration.

**Causes**

- ✓ concern about one's health.
- ✓ A close relative of the nosophobic passed away from an uncurable disease.
- ✓ Other behavioural problems, such as bipolar disorder, schizophrenia, severe depression, or obsessive-compulsive disorders, may increase a patient's fear of serious disease.
- ✓ Nosophobia may be brought on by a somatic amplification disorder, a condition connected to perception and cognition.
- ✓ The nosophobic in this instance has unfavourable feelings about the idea of being ill.
- ✓ Excessive fear of being sick might be brought on by reading articles online or watching television programmes about incurable diseases.
- ✓ Major worldwide illness outbreaks like the COVID-19 pandemic may cause people to develop phobias.

# 107. Nostophobia, ecophobia -fear of returning home

Nostophobia, commonly referred to as "ecophobia," is an extreme dislike or fear of returning to one's home. The house might not always be the source of this anxiety. One of the fears that might be triggered by going home is the perception of failure

One of the fears that might be triggered by going home is the perception of failure.

**Symptoms / signs**

- Worry while considering home
- Severe fear and nervousness within or around their house.
- *Escaping their house constantly*
- Incapable of managing their anxieties.
- Possibly prone to panic attacks

**Causes**

- Family violence is another phobia-inducing factor.
- The student has failed or received a lower grade and is afraid to return home.
- Fear of returning home
- Fear of family members
- Work imbalance and high family expectations.

# 108. Numerophobia -fear of all numbers

Extreme fear of numbers is known as "numerophobia. People could be scared of all the numbers or just a few. Arithmophobia is another name for it. A person with numerophobia may be afraid of any numbers, particularly those used in difficult mathematical calculations. The person may experience severe terror at the mere notion of doing calculations in daily life or answering a challenging math problem in class.

**Symptoms / Signs**

- A child with numerophobia may exhibit avoidance behaviour, crying or screaming at the idea of going to school (Didaskaleinophobia).
- Anxiety attacks can cause you to sweat a lot, feel like hiding or running away, have a fast heart rate, and breathe quickly.

**Causes**

- ✓ The phobic may often be able to deal with numbers, but they may do it with intense fear.
- ✓ Numerophobia is a common symptom of arithmophobia. The phobic may get overwhelmed when they see numbers on a calendar, the phone, or in notes with written dates. Tipping in restaurants or grocery shopping, where one must add up the prices of products, can be difficult for the phobic.

## 109. Nyctophobia- fear of darkness

Nyctophobia is a strong fear of the dark. Although it may afflict individuals of various ages, this fear is extremely prevalent among children. People who suffer from this particular anxiety condition may have difficulties falling asleep, have panic attacks, and fear going outside after dark.

**Symptoms or signs that make you nervous are**

- Entering a dimly lit area (like a movie theatre).
- Preparing for bed.
- Watching the sun set.
- Imagining being trapped in the dark.
- Trying to get some sleep at night.
- Keeping lights off.

**Causes**

- ✓ Your culture may also have an impact on your fear of the night and the dark.
- ✓ The stories you hear or read and the events you watch on television or in movies
- ✓ You worry about what could occur in the dark since you've heard or seen horrible things occur to other people in the same setting.

# 110. Obesophobia -fear of gaining weight

Obesophobia is a severe, paralyzing fear of gaining weight or becoming fat. It is an anxiety disorder called a particular phobia, or fear. Another name for it is pocrescophobia.

**Signs/symptoms**

- When you have obesophobia, your anxiety goes up when you talk about or think about gaining weight.
- Some individuals could have been brought up to think that gaining weight is wrong or repulsive.

**Causes**

- ✓ Environment: Some cultures tend to place too much emphasis on a person's appearance and weight.
- ✓ Genes: If you or someone in your family has a history of phobias, eating disorders, or other anxiety-related diseases, you may be more likely to have obesophobia.
- ✓ Traumatic encounters: Life events might cause obesophobia. One example is when a parent or other adult frequently tells a child that they are obese. An additional example might be a young bully making fun of someone's weight.

# 111.Oikophobia -fear of home surroundings and household appliances

The fear of one's immediate environment is called oikophobia or ecophobia. A particular phobia, such as Oikophobia or Ecophobia, is an overwhelming fear of anything within the home or of one's surroundings that might cause harm or death, together with the understanding that the fear is unreasonable, unnecessary, or excessive.

**Signs / Symptoms:**

- The fear of household injury-causing objects like gas heaters, stoves, and other appliances
- Ecophobia, as a generic term, describes a fear of domestic objects.
- Oikophobia is a term that is also used to describe homophobia, a condition in which the victim has a paralyzing fear of homes or being within one.

**Causes:**

A child may have seen an accident or a fatality, or they may have experienced an earthquake that destroys lives and property. Oikophobia, a persistent fear of being inside a home, might result from this.

## 112.Odontophobia-Fear of Dentist

- Odontophobics fear going to the dentist. When thinking about visiting the dentist or while at the dentist's office, a person with dentophobia may experience intense anxiety.
- It is usually a result of prior poor dental or medical experiences. The issue is that delaying dental visits often results in what has been referred to as the "vicious cycle of odontophobia."

## 113.Ommetaphobia-Fear of eyes

Severe fear of eyeballs is referred to as ometaphobia. This kind of fear, like other phobias, is illogical since there is no "actual" threat, yet it may be so intense that it affects your everyday life and social interactions.

**Signs / Symptoms :**

- However, "irrational" it may seem to others, ommetaphobia is quite genuine to people who experience it. To overcome ommetaphobia, you must first determine what is causing it. Coping techniques combined with therapy and potential drugs might be beneficial.

- A traumatic prior event involving the eyes in some form is likely the cause of an eye fear. As a result, certain eye-related conditions may very likely be the cause of this form of phobia.
- The first step is to determine the source of your agoraphobia. Seeing a mental health specialist can help you determine whether it is inherited or familial, related to social phobia, or even related to a traumatic prior experience.
- The unreasonable fear of dreams is known as oneirophobia. A person with this illness might anticipate experiencing an extremely high level of anxiety just by daydreaming.

**Causes**

✓ Their worry may even be so severe that it causes them to have a full-blown panic attack. Even though not every person with oneirophobia will experience such a surge of anxiety, it is still highly possible that they will.

✓ There are no known causes or effective therapies for oneirophobia, just as there are no known symptoms of this disorder. But there are still several treatments that may help a lot with some of the symptoms of oneirophobia.

# 114.Ophidiophobia-Fear of Snakes

Ophidiophobia is a severe, paralysing aversion to snakes. Specific phobia, a kind of anxiety illness, is the name of the ailment. Herpetophobia (fear of all reptiles) and ophidiophobia are possibly related.Snakes cause some level of anxiety in many individuals.

**Signs / Symptoms**

- Phobia sufferers frequently experience panic attacks.When exposed to snakes, they may also suffer a sudden, overwhelming sense of fear, anxiety, and panic. Even though they are not physically in the presence of snakes, they are terrified.
- When viewing snakes, experiencing fear or worry.
- Imagining snakes only when one is present being reluctant or unenthusiastic about being close to or touching a snake
- Adapting to seeing snakes in zoo enclosures and not changing one's behaviour to avoid coming into contact with them or to dislike or be repulsed by them

**Causes**

- ✓ Possibility of ophidiophobia in a relative's family.
- ✓ a person who has had a terrible snake bite.
- ✓ The fear of snakes (herpetophobia) or the dread of cats (thanatophobia) may be shared by someone close to the individual (fear of death due to snake bites).
- ✓ An individual has underlying mental health issues like panic disorder, anxiety disorder, etc.
- ✓ A person's dread of snakes may be sparked by their affiliation with a culture or religion that portrays them unfavourably.

# 115.Ophthalmophobia- fear of being stared at

- An anxiety condition called ophthalmophobia is defined by a pathological fear of being seen by others or seen in public.
- Erythrophobia, the fear of blushing, and an epileptic's fear of attention, which might trigger an episode, are two phobias that are similar to each other. In addition to being often linked to schizophrenia and other mental diseases, scopophobia The symptoms of scopophobia often overlap with those of other anxiety disorders. Scopophobia is regarded as a unique phobia as well as a social phobia.
- Treatment options are numerous.One treatment method, desensitisation, involves staring at the patient for a lengthy time as they express their sensations. The person is expected to either get desensitised to being seen or learn the cause of their ophthalmophobia.

## 116. Ornithophobia-Fear of Birds

- A fear of birds is called ornithophobia. You could become afraid of birds if you have a traumatic encounter with them.
- There are birds all over the place. A mental health professional might provide assistance if you discover that you avoid locations with birds and prefer to remain indoors. Exposure therapy is one kind of treatment that might help you progressively get over this phobia and appreciate nature.
- Make an appointment with a mental health specialist to learn how to deal with your fears.One approach or a mix of methods may be used during treatment.
- People who have a particular phobia could also take precautions to deal with their anxiety. For instance, a person with ornithophobia could decide not to visit a nearby park where there are many pigeons or ducks.

# 117.Osmophobia-Fear of Smell

- The word "osmophobia" refers to a fear of, dislike for, or aversion to smells or scents.
- Even though people who get migraines often say that smells bother them, the link between osmophobia and migraines has not been well studied.

# 118.Ostraconophobia- fear of shellfish

The unreasonable fear of shellfish is known as ostraconophobia. In the presence of shellfish, a person with this disease may get very anxious. They could find them really disgusting and hideous. They could even have full-blown panic episodes as a consequence of their ostraconophobia, depending on how severe their illness is.

- Their strong dislike of shellfish usually includes all kinds, like lobsters, crabs, shrimp, crayfish, and so on. Even being close to someone else while they eat shellfish may be difficult for them due to their extreme anxiety.
- Ostraconophobia is not known to have any recognised causes. However, a person's environment and genetics may have a big impact. Ostraconophobia may be more likely to develop in someone with a family history

of mental illness, particularly anxiety disorders or phobias.

## 119.Panphobia- Fear of everything

Panphobia, sometimes known as the Fear of Everything, is most likely a manifestation of the sufferer's "dismay" at being fearful in general rather than a true fear of everything.Panphobia is often used as a metaphor for "worry about many of things" rather than "everything," since this seems exceedingly improbable.

This is not always the case, however, since phobic reactions may also be inherited as acquired behaviours from the social setting in which they were raised. Panphobia may be the outcome of past traumatic events that can be directly (or indirectly) related to the object or situational fear.

**Symptoms:**

- Experience a sensation of impending doom that overwhelms you
- Go to tremendous measures to avoid anxiety-provoking situations
- Startle easily, find it difficult to relax, or have difficulties falling asleep
- You start experiencing headaches, tummy pain, or chest pain
- Frequently feel exhausted
- Most people frequently suffer occasional feelings of anxiety.

- Even those who don't regularly experience anxiety may do so occasionally - particularly if you experience a traumatic life event like losing your job or being gravely ill.

**Causes:**

- ✓ A significant factor is the family history. You may be more likely to acquire an anxiety condition or phobia if you have certain genes from your parents.
- ✓ Women are more likely than men to suffer from anxiety disorders.
- ✓ The chance of having an anxiety condition or phobia is increased by childhood maltreatment and trauma.

# 120.Pedophobia-Fear of children

People who have pedophobia have an unreasonable fear of infants and young children. A person with pedophobia may go to great lengths to avoid being near young children.This phobia is brought on by seeing or thinking about kids or babies. It is a feeling of fear, contempt, dislike, or prejudice towards children or young people. In certain contexts, pedophobia is synonymous with ephebiphobia.

Psychiatrists have been able to identify and treat children's fears, and studies have been done to look at how different treatments work. According to studies, fear of children may have an impact on a person's ability to conceive biologically.

## 121. Phagophobia- fear of swallowing

Phagophobia, or the fear of swallowing, is a psychogenic dysphagia. It manifests as a variety of swallowing issues without any obvious physical cause that may be found by physical examination and laboratory testing. It was claimed that the phrase "choking phobia," which is no longer used to describe this disease, is misleading and that it is vital to differentiate between the fear of swallowing and the fear of choking.

Fear is often misdiagnosed as an eating disorder because people don't eat as much as they should, which makes them lose weight.It is classified as a "particular phobia" under "anxiety disorders" in the Diagnostic and Statistical Manual of Mental Disorders, Fifth Edition.

## 122. Phallophobia-Fear of erection

Phaeophobia is often lumped in with other erotophobias or sexual phobias, such as coithophobia (fear of sexual interactions), gymnophobia (fear of nudity), and haphaephobia (fear of contact or being touched). It is usually called a sexual phobia because many people with it, especially women, avoid sexual activity to avoid the thing that makes them feel scared. Yet, this kind of phobia can affect both men and women.

Both flaccid and erect penises are the objects of irrational fear (medortophobia). Most people are aware that the penis, whether erect or not, is a natural object. Yet, some men and women are terrified of thinking about, seeing, or possessing an erect penis. This can be quite uncomfortable for many phobic individuals, making them avoid these uncomfortable circumstances.

Phallophobia is a fear of the male sexual organ that makes some people avoid it and can even cause them to lose control in an instant. It might be argued that both men and women can experience it.

**Symptoms**

Although this anxiety can initially seem strongly tied to a chapter on sexual assault, this is not the case.

The symptoms I just described could change based on the situation. There are three things to think about:

1. State of mind
2. degree of fear
3. Personality type

The phallophobic person may fully avoid sexual activity, but they may also experience anxiety attacks in situations like being seen naked, giving a passionate kiss, or even thinking about getting pregnant.In this way, a sequence of uncomfortable symptoms starts to appear when one is exposed to the male genital organ or an image of it:

- Absence of sex motivation
- excessive perspiration
- Anxiety attacks
- Panic episode
- loss of information
- Some people are classified as asexuals because they don't think they can ever feel sexual attraction. Although some people could view this as a sign of phallophobia, it is not the same. According to him, phallophobic people can be extremely scared just by thinking about thinking or by looking at a video or picture.
- Most people agree that phobias are caused by both internal factors (like heredity or genetics) and external factors (like traumatic events), but that the internal factors have a much bigger effect. This means that many phobias have their roots in a past triggering event, typically a traumatic incident that happened while a person was young. A negative sexual relationship in the past, for example, that caused the person with photophobia a lot of anguish, could be the source of the condition.

**Causes**

The reasons for phallophobia might differ from person to person, just like the symptoms do. The majority of the time, this suffering happens in childhood, when a person is most vulnerable to terror.

✓ **Sexual assault**

Sexual assault, specifically assault by an older male, is a common cause.Those close to the children, such as members of their own family, are frequently the men who abuse them.Apart from making men fear their penises, this reality also makes them seriously lack confidence, which over time may make it very difficult to build connections with males.

✓ **Painful sex encounters**

Due to highly painful sex, many people experience sexual disorders. In this way, the connection between the current physical discomfort and the male reproductive system can cause an overwhelming fear of the penis and a resulting loss of sexual desire.

✓ **A low sense of self**

Those with poor self-confidence may occasionally have reduced levels of sexual desire (low self-esteem). In the most severe cases of insecurity, the person may experience dread or panic in front of the opposing sex and its sexual organ.

## 123.Pharmacophobia- fear of medications

Pharmacophobia is a fear of medications and a disapproval of all pharmaceuticals. When people with pharmacophobia think about taking medicine, they have a wide range of symptoms, such as heart palpitations, panic attacks, fast heart rates, trembling, nausea, and even weakness.

**Symptoms:**

- Intense anxiety around drugs
- Anxiety when thinking about drugs
- Refusal to take medication
- may be in denial about their illness.
- Unable to cope with strong emotions
- May experience panic attacks.
- Muscle tension and shakiness

**Causes**

There is no known cause of pharmacophobia. However, genetics and one's environment may both play very significant roles.

# 124.Phasmophobia- fear of ghosts or phantoms

Philosophy is a paranoid fear of ghosts.Those who have a ghost phobia may experience irrational anxiety at the mere mention of supernatural creatures like ghosts, witches, or vampires.

It can be challenging to diagnose phantophobia, or the fear of ghosts. When sharing ghost stories or viewing films that include ghosts and other supernatural beings, many individuals get a rush of apprehension. The majority are able to regulate this fear, and some even like the sensation it produces.

**Symptoms**

- Difficulty sleeping
- Fear of being alone
- Intense fear of ghosts
- Difficulty sleeping alone
- Intense anxiety
- A great sense of dread or impending doom,
- Not using the bathroom at night,
- Daily tiredness from lack of sleep,
- Loss in productivity,
- Panic attacks, and difficulties sleeping alone are all symptoms.

**Causes**

- ✓ Phobophobia is an example of a phobia that can be caused by both genes and the environment.
- ✓ the connection between hypothyroidism and stress in the family
- ✓ a terrible event that occurred when the victim was a child;
- ✓ Viewing horror films and TV shows
- ✓ The impact of other phobias:

# 125. Philophobia-Fear of Love

Philophobia, or the fear of falling in love, may make it difficult for you to form lasting relationships. If you had a devastating breakup, divorce, abandonment, or rejection as a kid or adult, it's possible that you're now terrified to fall in love.

**Symptoms**

- Be unable to have intimate relationships.
- You experience extreme anxiety when in a relationship and constantly worry about the relationship ending.
- Feel afraid of your partner or their emotions.
- push people away or end relationships abruptly.
- Inability to initiate and maintain intimate relationships

- A constant fear of losing the current partner or ending relationships abruptly
- Never-ending feelings of insecurity and inferiority in a relationship

**Causes**

- ✓ Previous traumatic relationship: If a person has experienced a traumatic breakup, lengthy divorce proceedings, infidelity, or abuse, they can find it difficult to feel loved or maintain a relationship. Children also experience the same when they witness parents arguing, dying, or being abandoned.
- ✓ Increase in cultural and religious pressure:
- ✓ Rejection or abandonment: Lack of validation, attention, and love during childhood and adulthood can lead to philophobia.
- ✓ Disinhibited social engagement disorder (DSED)

# 126.Phyllophobia-fear of leaves

This fall, coulrophobia, the fear of clowns, may make more headlines than phyllophobia, the fear of leaves. But other individuals are afraid of those dead, crinkly leaves wherever they are.For a lot of people who have phyllophobia of leaves. Since they may just ignore the source of their anxiety, don't always feel the need for therapy. This helps those who are Phyllophobic feel in control of the situation. But sometimes, it could not be feasible or sufficient to avoid the leaves.

It is crucial for someone to constantly look for expert assistance when it is available. In this manner, you don't waste time, work more, and comprehend what is going on. After gaining insight, you may work on conquering your phobia of leaves.

# 127.Phobophobia- fear of fear itself

The severe fear of being terrified is known as phobophobia. Even though it may seem redundant, this ailment is a very genuine and complicated disorder that may manifest in a variety of ways. A person who suffers from phobophobia may be afraid of the physical symptoms of fear, such as chest pain, sweaty palms, or irregular heartbeat.

Internal tendencies are mostly responsible for phobias. It is created by the unconscious mind and is connected to a phobia-inducing incident that included emotional trauma and stress, two factors that are directly related to anxiety disorders, as well as forgetting and remembering the initial trauma.

It's difficult to estimate the precise number of individuals who have a particular phobia, like phobophobia, although it's uncommon. However, we do know that 1 in 10 American adults and 1 in 5 adolescents will have a particular phobia condition at some time in their life.

# 128.Phonophobia- fear of loud sounds or voices

A persistent, unnatural, and unfounded fear of sound is known as phonophobia. Frequently, these are everyday sounds from the surroundings like traffic, kitchen noises, doors shutting, or even loud speaking, none of which may ever be harmful.

It could result from hereditary reasons. Anxiety problems run in families; therefore, certain people may be more susceptible to this illness. External factors, such as a history of sustained childhood stress or a single traumatic event, might also contribute to phonophobia. It is an extremely uncommon phobia that often results from hyperacusis.

## 129.Pogonophobia-Fear of beards

A severe phobia of beards is known as pogonophobia. The name "Pogon" is derived from the Greek meaning beards. A person with pogonophobia could experience intense fear or panic while around others who have beards. They might experience the same emotions if they see a picture or video of someone sporting a beard.

Extreme anxiety, shortness of breath, rapid heartbeat, sweating, trembling, and a full-blown panic attack are just a few of the serious pogonophobia symptoms that can occur. Pogonophobic individuals may also have negative effects on their social and professional lives. People with pogonophobia may find it difficult to function at work or in social situations where they will frequently interact with people with beards if being around them causes an extreme reaction.

# 130.Pornophobia-Fear of Nudity

Pornophobia is the fear of pornography, or it may also frequently be the fear of overusing porn. Those who hold the opinion that pornographic materials are "bad," "unethical," or otherwise negative are likely to have had an impact on people who develop a fear of pornography.

In that it is an "over-exaggerated" dislike of pornographic images or movies, pornophobia is somewhat the opposite of porn addiction. While the frightened circumstance or item may appear "ridiculous" or "silly" to others, the person who has pornophobia is all too aware that the nervous sensations they experience are quite genuine.

## 131.Porphyrophobia- fear of the colour purple

An extreme phobia of purple is called porphyrophobia. Some individuals get extreme anxiety or panic episodes when they see the hue. A person with porphyriphobia may avoid places like parks, gardens, shops, or any other place where they could run across purple items.

Porphyrophobia may have a significant impact on your mental health, much like other phobias. Being unable to anticipate when or where you may encounter the colour purple makes it challenging to go about regular activities. Panic attacks may result from a fear of porphyria.

People who have a fear of the colour purple may stay away from any setting where they could see it. To avoid seeing eggplants or plums, individuals may refuse to enter establishments with purple signage or avoid the produce section of supermarkets. To lessen the likelihood of seeing purple flowers like lavender or violets, they would even stay away from parks or gardens.

## 132.Pteromerhanophobia-Fear of flying

The fear of flying, or being in an aircraft or other flying vehicle, is known as pteromerhanophobia.

As of 2016, nothing was known about the causes of flying fear and the ways that it is perpetuated. It is unclear if there is only one condition or whether there are more. It seems that some individuals develop aerophobia due to a claustrophobia of tiny spaces, such as those found within an aircraft or helicopter's fuselage.

They will do everything in their power to avoid flying, which results in severe anguish and impairs their capacity to operate. The parts of flying that seem to cause the greatest anxiety are take-off, severe weather, and turbulence.

## 133.Pyrophobia-Fear of fire

Extreme fire phobia is known as pyrophobia. Those who suffer from pyrophobia may experience fear at the sight of any kind of fire, even a bonfire or candle flame. Or they could experience acute anxiety when they consider or discuss fire. Even when there isn't any actual threat or risk, they could anticipate fire in any location or circumstance.

Both cognitive behavioural therapy and exposure therapy are effective treatments for pyrophobia.

The fear of fire as a possible danger to life safety is the most frequent cause of pyrophobia (which is identical in animals). Extremely pyrophobic individuals, however, are unable to even approach or endure a modest controlled fire, such as a fireplace, bonfire, or lighted candle. In many instances, a negative fire experience as a Child may have set off the illness.

## 134.Radiophobia-Fear of Radiation / Xerox

Ionizing radiation fear is known as radiophobia. Patients who refuse to get X-rays because they think the radiation would kill them are only one example.

Since the 1945 atomic bombs of Hiroshima and Nagasaki, radiophobia has been thoroughly documented, but nothing has been done to address it.

High radiation doses should be feared since they may be dangerous and even fatal (e.g., radiation-induced cancer and acute radiation syndrome). The phrase is also used to refer to resistance to nuclear technology (i.e., nuclear power) based on worries that are much more significant than the actual hazards warrant.

# 135. Ranidaphobia-Fear of frogs

An extreme and unreasonable fear of frogs or toads is known as ranidaphobia. Specific phobia, which is a kind of anxiety disorder, is the condition. People who suffer from ranidaphobia may think frogs and toads might hurt them. They could also be concerned that amphibians would develop and supplant humans.

Ranidaphobia (from ranidae, the most frequent family of frogs) is a particular phobia of frogs and toads, as well as a pervasive superstition found in the folkways of many different civilizations. In place of any specific terminology, psychiatric specialty literature refers to "fear of frogs" in its basic form.

# 136.Scopophobia- fear of being looked at or stared at

An overwhelming fear of being seen is known as scopophobia. While it is common to experience anxiety or discomfort in circumstances when you are likely to be the focus of attention, such as while performing or speaking in front of an audience, scopolobia is more severe. You can get a sense of scrutiny.

The fear of being evaluated, ridiculed, or rejected by others is often a factor in scopophobia. This is a major sign of social anxiety disorder, but it may also be brought on by any concern one may have about how they seem, behave, or interact with others.

While many individuals experience some amount of fear when they are the focus of attention, for those who have scopophobia, these sensations are disproportionate to the scenario and are amplified.

## 137.Sexophobia -Fear of sexual Organs

Sexophobia is a fear of the sexual organs or of sexual activity. In a broader sense, it is a fear of sexuality.As a result, it may refer to widespread stigmatisation from collective organisations like religious groups, institutions, and/or governments, as well as a person's attitude based on their educational background, personal experience, and personality.

## 138.Siderodromophobia-Fear of Train

Siderodromophobia, sometimes known as the fear of trains, is a condition that encompasses all anxiety associated with trains. Some individuals worry about colliding, while others worry about losing control. Others report that although they do not specifically fear trains, other phobias like claustrophobia, social phobia, or germ phobia are triggered by them.

Though not always, the fear of becoming stranded on train tracks is connected to a bad memory. You may have a higher chance of developing a phobia if your automobile has ever stalled on the tracks. However, you do not need to have personally experienced the bad thing. A train will sometimes derail, or someone may be hit by an approaching train.

## 139.Social Phobia-Social anxiety

Social anxiety disorder or social phobia is a strong and long-lasting fear of being around other people.It's a typical issue that often manifests in adolescence. It may be really upsetting and significantly affect your life. Some individuals find that as they age, things get better.

Most people who have a social phobia are afraid of speaking in front of other people.Social phobias may often make individuals avoid social settings, such as those at work or school, which can negatively affect the person's well-being and capacity to function.

Kids who are bullied, teased, rejected, or put down in other ways may be more likely to have social anxiety disorder.In addition, this disease may be linked to other unfortunate life experiences such as family strife, trauma, or abuse.

## 140.Somniphobia-Fear of Sleep

Somniphobia is a severe phobia of sleeping. People who have this phobia could worry about having nightmares, going through sleep paralysis, or passing away while they are asleep. People with somniphobia often make an effort to put off going to bed as long as they can.

A common cause of somniphobia is a fear of having nightmares or going through sleep paralysis. Trauma survivors may also be more prone to developing somniphobia.

A history of parasomnia is the main risk factor for somniphobia. Chronic sleep-related issues called parasomnias include nightmares and sleep paralysis. Parasomniacs may experience anxiety before going to bed. They worry about suffering the sleep issues again, which makes them anxious.

## 141. Spectrophobia-Fear of Mirror

The fear of mirrors and/or the terror of what could be reflected in them is known as spectrophobia, a sort of anxiety illness that is categorised as a particular phobia. It is also known as catoptrophobia and eisoptrophobia. Those who suffer from spectrophobia may have intense phobias of their own reflection, the mirror itself, or spirits that appear in mirrors.

Despite being very uncommon, this illness may nevertheless be exceedingly dangerous. Similar to other phobias, spectrophobia may cause havoc in every area of a person's life and cause avoidance tactics. Having spectrophobia symptoms may be quite crippling and have an effect on one's general quality of life.Depending on your specific requirements, spectrophobia treatment may vary, but it usually includes some kind of psychotherapy. Even though receiving spectrophobia therapy might be intimidating or stressful, it's crucial to put your health first.

# 142.Stasiphobia-Fear or standing & walking

Stasiphobia, also referred to as the Fear of Standing, is a rare phobia that may result from problems with a person's balance system.The fear that you could faint or fall over if you stood up and injured yourself may be the source of your stasiphobia.

Stasiphobia sufferers will experience genuine fear, worry, and tension as long as they believe the situation or thing they fear will cause them harm, because our brains are more than capable of producing true bodily responses to any given scenario.

Stasiphobia has many of the same symptoms as other specific phobias, such as anger issues, social anxiety, panic attacks, tension, and depressive symptoms.

## 143. Submechanophobia-Fear of Manmade things

Fear of partially or completely submerged human-made items is known as submechanophobia. These artefacts may be from shipwrecks, monuments, animatronics from amusement parks, or historic structures, but they could also include more commonplace objects like buoys and other random rubbish.

Many people who suffer from submechanophobia have the same symptoms: extreme fear brought on by the idea of submerged man-made items, bodily pains, tense muscles, avoidance of areas where potential interaction with triggers is present, a lack of breath; and a feeling of choking.

Finding and dealing with the worries that are making the fear worse is usually the first step in treating a fear of man-made things that are underwater.If a patient feels that their disease is out of control and interfering with their daily lives, they may seek treatment.

## 144.Taphophobia- fear of graves

Taphophobia is an abnormal fear of being declared dead but then being buried alive. Most individuals are afraid of dying. Taphophobia, or any phobia for that matter, is more likely to develop in those who are already depressed or anxious.

In modern times, taphophobia is a very rare mental health problem. Other types of social anxiety disorders are much more common. The apprehension of organ donation from a patient who is still alive could be its contemporary counterpart.

## 145. Technophobia<br>Fear of advanced technology

Technophobia, often referred to as "techno fear," is the aversion or fear of cutting-edge technology or sophisticated gadgets, particularly computers.

Psychologists use cognitive-behavioral therapy or psychodynamic therapy to address technophobia. In cognitive behaviour therapy, you are trained to gradually confront your anxieties in order to eventually stop reacting to technology with aversion or anxiety.

Technophobia is the fear of using technology, and it may make a person feel anxious. They might: Hold off on purchasing a new phone or computer, and refuse to use card readers, computers, or ATMs Avoid using any automated systems, such as withdrawals made automatically to pay bills.

## 146. Telephone phobia -Fear of the phone

Telephone phobia, or "fear of telephones," is the hesitation or fear of making or receiving phone calls. It is thought to be a kind of social anxiety or social phobia.There is a broad range of intensity for the fear of phone calls and their accompanying challenges, as is typical with other fears and phobias. In 1993, about 2.5 million people in Great Britain were said to suffer from telephone phobia.These signs may include shaking, a racing heart, hot hands, shortness of breath, nausea, a dry mouth, and a tense stomach. The person who is suffering could feel fear, panic, and fear. Panic attacks can cause symptoms such as hyperventilation and anxiety.Both the act of making and receiving calls as well as the idea of doing so might result in these unpleasant and irritating sensations.

# 147.Teratophobia
# - fear of giving birth to a monster

Teratophobia is an unfounded fear of monsters, or the fear of being pregnant with a monster.Cognitive behavioural therapy may be used to address this utilising exposure and approaches for reducing fear. Many times, taking anti-depressant or anti-anxiety medication is beneficial, particularly in the beginning phases of treatment.

# 148.Tetraphobia- fear of the number 4

Tetraphobia is an irrational fear of the number four. It is common in China and Japan, as well as other east Asian countries.The explanation is rather straightforward; in many east Asian languages, the word for "four" really sounds extremely similar to the word for "death."

Most people with tetraphobia reside in China, Vietnam, Korea, and Japan. For Cantonese-speaking Chinese people, the numbers 4, 14, and 24 are symbolic of death since their respective words sound like the meanings for "death," "must die," and "easy to die," respectively.

# 149.Thalassophobia-Fear of Sea

An extreme phobia or fear of enormous bodies of water is called thalassophobia. Thalassophobia is a fear of the sea, the ocean, and the big lakes. Some people may have a slight fear of the sea. However, for certain people, sea phobia might be a far greater issue.

Traumatic experiences might also contribute to thalassophobia. A near-drowning incident in childhood, seeing a shark attack, never learning to swim, or simply hearing spooky ocean tales are just a few examples of probable triggers for thalassophobia.

Thalassophobia is often regarded as a unique form of phobia that occurs in a natural setting. One of the most prevalent sorts of phobias is fear of the natural environment, and some research indicates that women are more likely than men to develop phobias of the water

## 150. Thanatophobia- fear of intolerance to high temperatures

Thanatophobia is a severe fear of dying or death itself. While sometimes experiencing fear of death is normal, thanatophobia is an anxiety condition that may have a negative impact on many facets of your life. Do not be reluctant to discuss your worries with a healthcare professional.

The good news is that as people age, their fear of dying lessens. Men who developed thanatophobia in their 20s often overcame their phobia and are less likely to have negative feelings about the topic in the future. Women, on the other hand, are more likely than men to have the issue resurface in their 50s. A doctor could advise thanatophobia sufferers to get help for an anxiety condition, a phobia, or any particular underlying reason for their fear.

## 151.Thermophobia- fear of sea

The fear of high temperatures in either inorganic materials or living things is called thermophobia.Thermophobics endure anxiety while being aware that their fear is unfounded. They could remain indoors on warm days, wear light clothes, live in a cold region, avoid hot water, and avoid hot meals in order to prevent heat.

In the same way that there are no known causes or effective therapies for thermophobia, there are also no known symptoms of this disorder. However, there are a number of treatments that may help significantly reduce some of the symptoms of thermophobia.

## 152.Tokophobia- fear of Dying

Tokophobia is a pathological fear of becoming pregnant that makes people avoid giving birth.

It is either primary or secondary in nature.Primary tokophobia is a woman's obsessive fear of delivery when she has never been pregnant before. In adolescence or the early stages of adulthood, fear of childbirth may begin.

Sleep issues, panic attacks, nightmares, and avoidance behaviours are some of the signs of tokophobia. Up to 78% of women say they worry about getting pregnant and giving birth, but only 13% say their anxiety is so bad that it makes them delay or avoid trying to get pregnant. Women who have never given birth are more likely than those who suffer from tokophobia.

.

## 153.Tomophobia- fear of invasive medical procedure

Tomophobia is a term used to describe fear or anxiety caused by impending medical treatments or surgical procedures.After being told she has tomophobia, Lis says that psychotherapy is the best way to treat it.Cognitive-behavioral therapy (CBT), which includes altering thinking processes, is one effective approach to treating phobias.Tomophobia's actual root cause is not known. However, specialists have theories regarding what can cause someone to acquire a fear of medical procedures.

## 154. Tonitrophobia-Fear of Thunder

Tonitrophobia is a type of specific phobia that involves an abnormal fear of thunder and lightning or an irrational fear of scattered or isolated thunderstorms.It is a condition that both people and animals may get over. Tonitrophobia makes it very difficult for a person to cope with severe weather or storms. The likelihood of exceptionally loud thunder under such circumstances will cause a great deal of fear.Tonitrophobia has no known cause. However, a person's environment and genetics may have a significant impact on the development of this illness.

## 155.Toxiphobia-Fear of being Poisoned

The unreasonable fear of poisons and being poisoned is known as toxicity. Although individuals have been poisoned in different crimes throughout the past, it is quite unusual and hence the fear may be tied more to paranoia or paranoid thinking issues.Toxiphobia is the rejection of foods with tastes, odours, or appearances that are followed by illness brought on by toxins found in those foods in non-human animals. Toxiphobia, or the irrational fear of poisons and being poisoned, affects both humans and animals.

## 156. Traumatophobia-Fear of Injury

Traumatophobia is an abnormal fear of combat, conflict, or being hurt when participating in physical activities like sports. When injury-related scenarios cause anxiety and tension, you could have traumatophobia. A second injury is a major source of anxiety. When you have traumatophobia, you could replay the trauma and suffering of your injury as your anxiety grows about experiencing it again.Exposing the patient to the stimuli , in this example, exposure to blood, damage, and injections, and repeating the procedure until the patient's responses are lessened or the condition is healed, is one type of behavioural treatment for traumatophobia. Another option is hypnotherapy.

# 157.Trichophobia-Fear of Hair loss

Trichophobia is a morbid fear of hair or diseases affecting the hair. Some researchers believe it may arise from stress or anxiety. depression or other mental health conditions, such as trichotillomania. obsessive-compulsive disorder

If your fear of hair is starting to take over your life, there is help. While trichophobia is considered rare (Trusted Source), experts estimate that specific phobias affect between 7 and 9 percent of the population. Physical symptoms might include an increased heart rate, hot or cold flashes, difficulty breathing, dizziness, or lightheadedness.

# 158.Triskaidekaphobia-Fear of No.13

Trichodekaphobia is an extreme or irrational fear of the number 13, which is commonly associated with bad luck in Western culture.While fear of the number 13 can be traced back to mediaeval times, the word "triskaidekaphobia" itself is of recent vintage.

Most people with triskaidekaphobia find that their fear only arises in certain situations, and does not significantly impair their lives.

## 159.Trypanophobia- fear of needles or injections

Trypanophobia is a strong aversion to needles. Specifically, people with trypanophobia fear needles in medical settings. They may avoid getting vaccines, blood draws, or intravenous (IV) fluids. Although needle phobia is common, it can have severe consequences if it causes you to avoid or delay medical care.

According to estimates, as many as 2 in 3 children and 1 in 4 adults are afraid of needles. As many as 1 in 10 people might delay the COVID-19 vaccine due to these fears. Many people grow out of trypanophobia, but many adults still fear needles. According to some reports, up to 16% of adults avoid getting vaccines because they're afraid of needles. Other studies show that up to 1 in 10 adults struggle with needle phobia.

People with trypanophobia have intense anxiety at the sight or thought of a procedure involving a needle. Sometimes, this anxiety is so severe that it's debilitating. It may lead to a panic attack.

# 160.Trypophobia-Fear of Holes

Trypophobia is a strong fear of holes or textures with a pattern of holes, as well as a dislike of densely packed holes.People with this phobia tend to feel sick, disgusted, and upset when they look at surfaces with lots of small holes close together or in a pattern.

Scientists haven't been able to find a clear reason for trypophobia yet, but there are a few possibilities.The fear of holes, then, may be less a fear of holes and more an unconscious association of harmless items (like lotus seed pods) with feared animals (like a blue-ringed octopus) because they share certain spectral features.

Only mental health professionals can diagnose phobias, like a fear of holes. Since there's no official diagnosis of trypophobia, a therapist won't diagnose it specifically.

# 161.Vehophobia-Fear of Driving

Vehophobia, which is a fear of driving, is quite common, both in people who have been involved in serious accidents and sometimes even in those who have not. Many people who suffer from vehophobia choose not to drive altogether because the anxiety and fear are so overwhelming.

"The most common cause of vehophobia is being involved in a motor vehicle accident and being afraid of getting back out there." Other factors that can contribute to vehophobia include witnessing a serious car accident or seeing a bad accident on the news or social media. Growing up with parents who were always anxious in the car.

If a person was in a serious accident while driving and was injured or caused an injury to another, they could develop a fear of driving as a result. The same could happen even if they were a passenger in the car. The treatment options for a driving phobia are straightforward and effective. By using cognitive behavioural therapy (CBT) combined with anxiety medication, if needed, symptoms can quickly improve and create lasting change.

## 162.Verminophobia-Fear of Germs

It is an extreme fear of germs. You may go out of your way to avoid situations that expose you to germs. The phobia and the steps you take to avoid it worsen over time. You may find yourself stuck in a cycle of repetitive behaviours that affect your quality of life, similar to obsessive-compulsive disorder (OCD).

Behaviors that can affect your daily life include: washing your hands often, several times in a row, or for an unusually long time, always wearing gloves to prevent contact with germs, covering items you use daily, such as remote controls or the steering wheel of your car.

It's also possible to lower the risk of mysophobia by taking good care of your mental health. You can do this by: limiting alcohol and recreational drug consumption, taking up a new hobby to take your mind off germs and other stressors, and spending time with loved ones.

.

## 163.Workplacephobia- fear of the workplace, a subset of ergophobia

Workplace phobia is defined as a phobic anxiety reaction with symptoms of panic occurring when thinking about or approaching the workplace. People suffering from workplace phobia regularly avoid confrontation with the workplace and are often on sick leave.

In the self-rating of workplace phobia, people with workplace phobia scored much higher than people with other types of anxiety disorders.A similar significant difference was not found concerning the general psychosomatic symptom load.

Talking with a mental health professional can help you manage your specific phobia. Exposure therapy and cognitive behavioural therapy are the most effective treatments. Exposure therapy focuses on changing your response to the object or situation that you fear.

# 164.Xanthophobia- fear of the colour yellow

xanthophobia is an aversion to yellow light; it is the irrational fear of the color yellow. Someone suffering from this condition can expect to experience a very high amount of anxiety from merely thinking of the color yellow.

In fact, their worry might be so bad that they might even have a full-blown panic attack. Even though not everyone with xanthophobia will experience this kind of increase in anxiety, it is still very possible that it will happen.

When a person with xanthophobia has a full-blown panic attack, they will likely have a faster heart rate, faster breathing, higher blood pressure, tight muscles, trembling, and a lot of sweating, among other things.Although panic attacks may not always be the case for everyone experiencing symptoms of xanthophobia, it is still possible for them to occur, especially if their symptoms are very severe.

## 165. Zoophobia- fear of animals

Zoophobia is an extreme fear of animals. Many people who have zoophobia fear one specific type of animal. Others fear many types of animals or all animals. The fear of animals is a type of anxiety disorder called a "specific phobia. Specific phobias are intense fears of certain objects, situations, people, or animals.

The exact cause of zoophobia isn't known. It's possible that several factors could contribute to the development of the condition, including negative experiences. Having a negative experience with an animal may cause you to fear it.A strong fear of something is one of the main signs of a specific phobia. Most of the time, this fear is bigger than the threat that the object of fear poses.

Thank you

Dr. Y. Narasimha Raja

Mrs. Y. Sree Lakshmi